Books are to be returned on the last date below.

2008

DETECTIVE STORIES

TRUE SPY STORIES

Terry D...

Illustrated by
David Wyatt

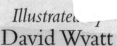

D1642653

EVERETT LIBRARY

J05822F1848

The facts behind these stories are true. However, they have been dramatized in order to give a gripping account of the way they might have happened; some of the characters are fictitious.

Scholastic Children's Books,
Commonwealth House, 1-19 New Oxford Street,
London WC1A 1NU, UK

A division of Scholastic Ltd
London ~ New York ~ Toronto ~ Sydney ~ Auckland
Mexico City ~ New Delhi ~ Hong Kong

Published in this edition by Scholastic Ltd, 2002

True Detective Stories
First published in the UK by Scholastic Ltd, 1996
Text copyright © Terry Deary, 1996
Illustrations copyright © David Wyatt, 1996

True Spy Stories
First published in the UK by Scholastic Ltd, 1998
Text copyright © Terry Deary, 1998
Illustrations copyright © David Wyatt, 1998

ISBN 0 439 97812 2

All rights reserved
Printed by Cox & Wyman, Reading, Berks

2 4 6 8 10 9 7 5 3 1

The right of Terry Deary and David Wyatt to be identified as author and illustrator of this work respectively has been asserted by them in accordance with the Copyright, Designs and Patents Act, 1988.

This book is sold subject to the condition that it shall not, by way of trade or otherwise be lent, resold, hired out, or otherwise circulated without the publisher's prior consent in any form of binding or cover other than that in which it is published and without a similar condition, including this condition, being imposed on a subsequent purchaser.

TRUE

DETECTIVE

STORIES

CLASS:	F : DEA	
No. J		
AUTHOR	SUBJECT	DATE
		1996
	-	AUG 2005
		£4.99

For Rosemary Bromley, who deserves more than 100% of the credit

CONTENTS

INTRODUCTION

Sherlock Holmes never solved a mystery.

Hercule Poirot never cracked a crime.

Columbo never caught a crook.

Miss Marple never unmasked a murderer.

Why not? Because they, and a hundred other famous detectives, are all characters invented by writers. Detective stories are great fun. They are puzzles for you to solve, they are exciting adventures to enjoy, they are crimes to chill you and mysteries to entertain you. But if you're ever the victim of a *real* crime it's no use looking for one of these clever detectives in the *Yellow Pages*. You'll have to call the local police and have it investigated by a real detective.

The work of a real detective is rather different from that shown in books, films and television programmes. Not many people know the names of these real detectives the way they know the name of Sherlock Holmes. And not many people know their true stories.

Here is a collection of stories about real crime-crackers who have solved puzzles just as interesting as those investigated by heroes in books. Stories that are just as curious, chilling, mysterious and entertaining; stories from around the world from Australia to Britain; stories about police detectives . . . as well as some about amateur investigators who never expected to be solving a crime.

Some of the words spoken by the characters have been invented to make them easier to read as stories, but the cases are true and they were solved by real detectives. As well as the stories there are fact files to help you understand how crime investigators worked in the past and how they work now.

THE MAN WHO ROBBED HIMSELF

Police sometimes call on the help of experts to catch criminals. An expert can also produce evidence which will prove a suspect is not to blame. But what happens when the police and the expert disagree? Can the expert turn detective to prove his case?

Budapest, Hungary, 1938

Hanna Sulner sat down heavily at the restaurant table and looked at the man who was already seated there. "Sorry, Hary," she said, "I'm not going to be very good company today. I've had a bad, bad day."

Hary Erkel grinned. "So, you're going to take it out on me, yes?"

The young woman stuck out her tongue and pulled her straight dark eyebrows together in a scowl. "Why not? You're a man, and men think they know everything."

"We do," Hary said.

"You know *nothing*," Hanna said. "I am an expert. I am probably Hungary's greatest expert in the study of handwriting. The police call for my help a dozen times. But *this* time, when I give my opinion, they ignore me. They arrest an innocent man, destroy his wife's life and practically tell me I am a fool or a liar. Well, I am not mistaken. I just wish I knew how to prove it," she said.

"Who is this innocent man and what did he do?" Hary asked gently.

"He did nothing! That's what I'm telling you!" Hanna replied. One or two of the customers in the restaurant looked up from their meals to see what she was so agitated about. She lowered her voice. "His name is Miklos and he is accused of theft. He is the accountant for a small business in Budapest and he is paid 1000 forints a month.

10

When he left work on the Friday evening before Christmas there were half a million forints in the safe. When he returned after Christmas the safe was empty."

"How was the safe opened?" Hary asked.

"It had been opened by someone who knew the combination lock numbers. And only two people knew those numbers: Miklos and the owner. There was only one set of fingerprints on the safe —"

"Don't tell me," Hary cut in. "They belonged to Miklos."

"They did," Hanna said.

"That's what they call an open and shut case," Hary shrugged.

The young woman glared at him again. "Typical man, jumping to conclusions!" she hissed. "The police didn't think they had enough evidence to arrest him. They made enquiries at the Budapest banks and made an important discovery. On the Monday after the robbery a woman had paid nearly half a million forints into a bank account. She used the name Anna Nagy."

"A common enough name," Hary said.

"Unfortunately it was the name of Miklos's wife before she married him," Hanna said.

Hary thought carefully, in case he irritated the hand-writing expert any more. "The police supposed he'd given the money to his wife and she'd paid it into a bank, then?"

"They did," Hanna agreed. "And, to make things worse, they went around to Miklos's house and discovered they'd bought a lot of new things for Christmas: a new radio, a pram for the baby Anna was expecting, new furniture for the nursery and so on. They found receipts for 7,000 forints."

"It looks bad for Miklos," Hary muttered.

"The poor man had saved it! For four years, he'd been saving. Then they had a spending spree so they were all ready for the arrival of their first baby."

Hary picked up a menu and studied it. "You have to admit it looks a bit unlikely. The police have arrested people on less evidence than that."

Hanna nodded miserably. "Just soup for me. I'm not very hungry."

"This case has really upset you, hasn't it?" Hary said.

"Yes," she said, twisting the table napkin miserably. "Miklos has had the most amazing bad luck. There were just two people who could prove that his wife hadn't paid that money into the bank, and one of those people was the bank cashier, of course. There was every chance that he would remember what the mysterious Anna Nagy looked like and tell the police that it wasn't Miklos's wife."

"Don't tell me," Hary said. "He'd forgotten all about Anna Nagy."

"Worse," Hanna said. "He'd suffered a heart attack at Christmas and died."

"That *is* bad luck," Hary agreed. "So who was the other person who could prove Miklos's wife didn't make that payment?"

Hanna looked up. "Why, *me* of course. They had the paying-in slip for that half-million forints. It was signed 'Anna Nagy'. The police asked Miklos's wife to sign that name, then they gave both specimens to me to compare."

"Don't tell me. They were the same. His wife had done the robbery without telling him!" Hary laughed.

Hanna snapped, "Now you're being silly."

"Sorry," the young man said. "Tell me about it."

"The signatures were totally different. A blind person could see they were not written by the same person. They didn't need *me* to tell them that."

"But you did," Hary put in.

"But I did. The police didn't believe me . . . they didn't *want* to believe me. They said she had disguised her handwriting in case she was caught. Practically called me a liar. They pressed ahead with the charge and Miklos went to court yesterday."

Hary ordered the meal from a waiter and sat back in his chair. "They didn't call you as a witness, then?"

"The police didn't, but Miklos's lawyer did. I was able to tell them that the person who wrote that signature was a lot older than Miklos's wife. I was also able to tell them that she had some sort of physical problem with her writing, something that made writing difficult."

"But the court didn't believe you either?" Hary asked.

Hanna spread the napkin on her lap then crumpled it again. "The police had an answer for that. They said that Miklos's wife would be agitated when she wrote it . . . nervous about trying to cash in on her husband's crime. They also said they had checked on all the women in Budapest who are registered under the name of Anna Nagy – there were seven of them. They even put an advert in the newspapers for any other Anna Nagys to come forward if they had paid that money in legally. No one did."

Hary Erkel was fond of Hanna and didn't want to upset her. He didn't tell her what he was really thinking – that her kind heart was trying to see the good in the accountant and wouldn't admit that he was in fact a thief. "Your only hope would be if there was an Anna Nagy who was in

Budapest and was not registered."

"It's possible," the young woman said shortly.

"And if this Anna Nagy didn't read the papers," he added.

"That's possible too," she said defiantly.

"And if this Anna Nagy hasn't been back to the bank to touch any of that money?"

"Look, I saw his wife this morning," Hanna argued. "She's distracted! The baby's been born to a father who's in jail for theft. She's ill with worry."

Hary clicked his fingers. "Hey! Have you thought about that? You said the Anna Nagy who signed the bank slip had a physical problem. Could she have been ill?"

Hanna pulled a copy of the signature from her handbag and laid it flat on the tablecloth. She traced the shaking letters with her finger. "Yes, definitely, I should say."

"So have you checked the hospitals? Maybe someone came into Budapest from outside – someone who isn't registered here – and paid the money into the bank, then went to hospital for some reason."

Hanna's eyes widened. "Why didn't I think of that?" she whispered. "There are only four major hospitals in Budapest. I'll check them now." She jumped to her feet so quickly the white napkin fluttered to the floor.

"But your soup!" Hary cried.

Hanna didn't hear him. She was already out of the restaurant door and hurrying down the snow-dusted street.

The first hospital that Hanna tried raised her hopes cruelly. She was shown into a ward where an Anna Nagy lay in bed. The young Anna smiled at Hanna and showed her the twin babies proudly. "Yes, I am registered in Budapest and the police have already asked me about the bank account. Sorry . . . it's nothing to do with me. Best of luck," she said.

At the second hospital there was no Anna Nagy, but at the third the receptionist checked the list of names and said, "Yes, Ward 9. An old lady from Debrecen near the Romanian border."

"Will she see me?" Hanna said eagerly.

"Hah!" the receptionist snorted. "She'll see you, but she won't see you very well. She's nearly blind! She came to Budapest for an eye operation. Seems she's been saving for years to have it done. By all means go and have a chat with her. Second ward on the left, third bed on the right."

Hanna's heels clattered on the cold tile floors as she hurried towards Ward 9. The old woman in the third bed on the right seemed to be asleep. As Hanna sat in the wooden chair by the bedside it creaked and old Anna stirred.

"Is that you, nurse?"

"No. Mrs Nagy?"

"That's me."

"My name's Hanna Sulner. I'm from the university. I wondered if you could help me by answering a few questions?"

"I'll try. Just pass me that pair of spectacles, would you?" she said. "They don't help much yet but my eyes are getting better every day thanks to the doctors here. I'll be able to read again soon."

"Mrs Nagy," Hanna said as she passed the old woman the heavy glasses, "did you bring much money with you from Debrecen?"

"Nearly half a million forints," she replied, squinting through the glasses at the young woman.

"And you paid it into the National Bank on Bartok Street?"

"As soon as I arrived in Budapest," the old woman said.

"And that was when?"

"On Christmas Eve."

Hanna struggled to keep the tremble of excitement from her voice. "Mrs Nagy, I'll explain everything to you in a moment, but could I ask you to do just one thing for me? Would you sign your name on this blank slip of paper?"

"The signatures matched, of course," Hary Erkel said a week later. They were sitting in the same restaurant.

"Of course," Hanna said happily.

"You were right and the police were wrong."

"Of course. What else could you expect from a bunch of simple men?" she asked wickedly.

Hary looked a little hurt. "I seem to remember it was a simple man who gave you the idea of checking the hospitals for Anna Nagy."

Hanna Sulner was enjoying her meal this time. Her appetite had returned. "Some men are a little less stupid," she admitted, "but you don't get much more stupid than the police."

"They've released Miklos, haven't they?" he asked.

"That's not good enough," Hanna said. "They only released him because some of the evidence was weakened by finding the real Mrs Nagy. Miklos could still have stolen that money – people would still have suspected him. Mud sticks. The police had to find out who did steal the cash."

"So what is the answer?" Hary asked.

"Work it out for yourself," Hanna said playfully as she tore a piece from her bread roll and chewed it.

Hary dabbed at his mouth with the napkin to buy some time. Then a corner of his mouth turned up in a smile. It spread to his eyes. "Only two people knew the combination to the safe: Miklos and his boss. If Miklos didn't steal the money, then it must have been his boss!"

"That's what I told the police," Hanna said.

"You —"

"And they arrested Miklos's boss last night. He admitted everything. He crept back into the office over

17

that Christmas weekend. He wore gloves so he left no fingerprints. He opened the safe and took out the half-million forints. Then he claimed on the insurance and the insurance company paid him the half-million he said he'd lost!"

Hary gave a soft whistle. "He made a cool million forints by robbing himself! Miklos was lucky he had you on the case."

"No," Hanna frowned. "Miklos was very *unlucky*. Unlucky that his wife was born Anna Nagy, unlucky that the bank clerk died before the police could question him and unlucky that he chose to spend his savings at just the wrong time. Even the police might have solved the case quicker if it hadn't been for Miklos's bad luck."

"Or if they'd had you on the police force. You'd make a brilliant detective. Ever thought of joining the force?"

Hanna raised her glass of wine and sipped it. "Why should I?" she said and her eyes sparkled like the bubbling wine. "I'm already a brilliant hand-writing expert . . . for a woman."

FACT FILE

Fingerprints – FACT FILE

The police forces of the world rely heavily on experts to help with their detective work. Sometimes the experts are employed just when they are needed – doctors, for example. Others are employed as full-time policemen and women – fingerprint specialists or photographers.

Detectives can track down suspects but it is often the experts whose evidence leads to an arrest and a court conviction.

1. Fingerprints, those patterns of ridges on the tips of human fingers, are different for every human being. Even identical twins have different fingerprints.

2. Detectives always hope to find a fingerprint at the scene of a crime; if they can match it to the finger pattern of a suspect then they can prove that person was there, even if the criminal says he or she wasn't.

3. Fingerprints last for life or even longer. Egyptian mummies have fingerprints and they are 3,000 years old!

4. If the fingerprints are burned or rubbed off, the same pattern of prints will grow back. In 1934, the American gangster John Dillinger paid doctors to perform plastic surgery on his fingertips. It failed. Friends suggested he dip his fingers in acid. This worked for a while, but by the time he was caught the patterns reappeared. Another gangster, Robert Pitts, had skin transplanted from his chest to his fingertips. This got rid of the fingerprints but he was convicted on other evidence, and the doctor who operated on his fingers went to jail too!

5. The Ancient Chinese knew how to identify people from their fingerprints. They used a thumb print in wax as a 'signature' that couldn't be forged.

6. In 1892 the English scientist Sir Francis Galton wrote the first book on fingerprints. They were first used as evidence in the same year in a Brazilian murder case where the fingerprint was made in the victim's blood. Experiments then showed that fingers leave their invisible pattern on hard, smooth surfaces and special powder can be used to make the patterns show up. Police no longer had to hope the criminal would leave a visible print.

7. Millions of people have been convicted on

fingerprint evidence since that first case in 1892. In one classic case in 1948 the police in Blackburn, northern England, created a record when they fingerprinted 46,253 men to catch a killer.

8. It is possible to fake fingerprint evidence. In a 1943 case police in the Bahamas made an arrest after claiming they had found a fingerprint at a murder scene. Then the accused man's own private detective proved that the police had "transplanted" his print from a drinking glass to the scene of the crime. He was released.

9. The Federal Bureau of Investigation (FBI) of the United States keeps fingerprint records and now holds about 173 million people on its fingerprint files.

10. Fingerprints should be a foolproof way of proving someone is guilty (or innocent) of a crime. Unfortunately, fingerprint experts can make mistakes. Working eight hours a day, studying those tiny marks, needs great concentration. Mistakes have been made and innocent people have ended up in prison. Fingerprints may be foolproof but the people who read them aren't.

Fingerprints can't be copied easily. Hand-writing can. Police use handwriting

specialists (like Hanna Sulner) for advice, but don't consider their evidence to be absolute proof. Handwriting experts can often disagree with one another. That's what happened in a famous kidnapping case.

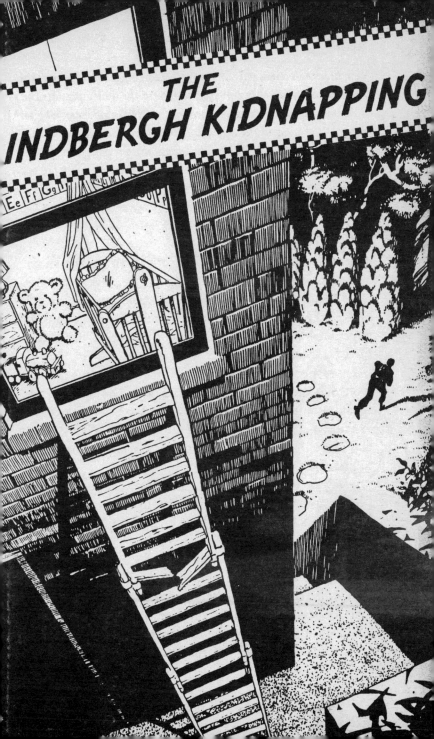

Sometimes detectives put a case together like a jigsaw. When all the pieces are in place they can see the face of the guilty person. But other, more ruthless, detectives see the face first, then go looking for pieces of jigsaw evidence that fit. If they find pieces that don't fit, they ignore them. And if they can't find the right pieces, they make them up. That may be what happened in America's most famous kidnapping case of all time.

USA, 1934

The man had a haunted look, the look of a man who knows he's going to die. And he was right.

"The jury found you guilty, Mr Hauptmann," I told him, pushing my hat to the back of my head. "You can't expect me to save you. I'm a private detective, not Marvo the Magician."

He turned away from the cold steel bars of his cell and looked at me. "I know that, Mr Elliot," he said quietly, speaking with a slight German accent. "I know they will execute me. They have to execute someone. They have to blame someone. All I want is for my friends and my family to know the truth."

"But the evidence against you was pretty convincing," I said. Something about the echo of my voice in that concrete cell made my flesh creep like a walk in a graveyard.

"The police did not give the full story in court," he said. No bitterness. Just a fact. I guess that's why I believed him. I guess also that I was the only person in the whole US of A who believed that Bruno Hauptmann might just be innocent of kidnapping the Lindbergh baby.

I'd read the newspapers, the same as everyone else. The

judge sure didn't believe in Hauptmann's innocence. Judge Quinn loved Hauptmann like Scrooge loved Christmas. His summing up was a work of art, the art of saying, "We all know he's guilty, so let's give him a fair trial – then execute him!"

What Quinn actually said was, "Charles Lindbergh is one of the heroes of the American people, the first man to fly solo across the Atlantic Ocean. He deserved a quiet and happy life with his wife and little son. Instead he found misery and heartbreak as the victim of one of the cruellest crimes of the century. Two years ago, on 1 March 1932, he said goodnight to his nineteen-month-old son Charles – or Buster as his loving parents called him. At 9.10 pm the Lindberghs heard a cracking sound from outside of the house – the sound we now know was the cracking of the kidnapper's ladder, the ladder that plays such an important part in this case. At 10 pm young Buster's nurse discovered an open shutter and little Buster gone from the nursery. She also saw a note on the windowsill. When the police opened it they found a ransom demand for $50,000. In the garden they found the ladder that had been used to reach the window. It was a home-made ladder, in three sections. Where the top section joined the second section the ladder had been broken – the noise the Lindberghs heard."

How Judge Quinn could know that was the noise they heard was beyond me, but no one challenged him. He went on to describe the ransom pick-up. A guy called John Condon offered to act as go-between for the Lindberghs. The kidnapper contacted Condon and sent him a letter – a letter full of spelling mistakes – and told the go-between to put an ad in the local paper when "the mony is redy".

Condon met the masked kidnapper twice. After the

first meeting the kidnapper sent the go-between Buster's babysuit to prove he had the kid. Then they met again in a graveyard and Condon handed over $50,000 in cash and gold certificates. It was one of those gold certificates that sank Hauptmann – the police had a note of all their numbers.

When Judge Quinn described the finding of Buster's dead little body he gave a performance that would have won him an Oscar in Hollywood. Finding Buster dead was the low point of the case for the police. Then, after two years of useless detective work, came the high point. Hauptmann handed over one of the $10 gold certificates for some petrol, the garage attendant made a note of the car number and the car was traced to Hauptmann.

I could see the judge's eyes glowing as he built up the case against Hauptmann. Once the police had a suspect they made all the evidence fit and it fitted like a glove. "Mr Hauptmann *says* he was given the money to look after by a friend," Judge Quinn said. He paused after the word "says". He left the jury in no doubt as to what he thought of Hauptmann's story. It's little pauses like that which will hang a man.

Then Judge Quinn reminded the jury about the ladder. A "wood technologist" called Koehler had traced where the wood for the rungs came from. The newspapers said it was "the greatest piece of scientific detection of all time". That wood was sold at a timber yard near to where Hauptmann lived. But the sixteenth rung – oh boy! That really put the final nail in the German's coffin. The police searched Hauptmann's attic and found that a floorboard had been ripped up and sawn. The wood matched the wood of rung 16. Four nail holes in the rung exactly fitted the nail holes of the missing floorboard! Brilliant detective work.

They didn't need any more evidence against Hauptmann, but Judge Quinn threw it in just to pour a few buckets of water over the drowning man. In the cell I tried that evidence on Hauptmann for size.

"You have a criminal record back in Germany," I told him. "That's why you ran away and came to America illegally."

"I was a burglar, not a kidnapper. I have committed no crimes in America."

"So where did the money come from? They found the Lindbergh kidnap money – or $14,000 of it – in your attic."

"Whose side are you on?" he said sharply. That made the guard look up and take a step towards him. "Sorry!" he said quickly.

"I'm on your side, Mr Hauptmann, but I need your side of the story. All I've heard so far is the case for the prosecution."

"Sure. Sorry," he muttered and sat down. "I made a good living as a carpenter. You could check my bank accounts – the police didn't bring them up in court. I was doing fine before the Lindbergh kidnap. I didn't need the money. Why would I want to risk my neck with a crime?"

"Answer my question," I said.

He sighed. "A friend called Fisch owed me 7,500 dollars when he went back to Germany. He left me a cardboard box to look after. It got damp in the attic, so I opened it to dry out whatever was in it. That's when I found the money."

"And helped yourself."

He spread his hard hands wide. "It was the money he owed me!"

"And it was also the Lindbergh kidnap money," I told him.

Hauptmann nodded. "The money was for sale in the Bronx area where we lived. For four dollars you could buy a ten-dollar gold bond – *if* you were willing to take the risk of getting caught spending it. Fisch must have bought those bonds, then left them with me until the case went out of the news."

"Nice friends you've got. Where's this Fisch now?"

The man looked down at the table. "I don't know. Somewhere in Germany."

"Have you tried to find him?"

"How could I when I'm locked up in here?"

"OK. So did the police try to find him?"

Hauptmann looked up angrily. "Why *would* they try?

They had me. All they were interested in was nailing me."

"And talking about nails, Mr Hauptmann, how do you explain the ladder?" I said, pushing him hard now he was getting angry. Angry men tell the truth.

"What about the ladder?" he asked.

"Made with wood from your local wood yard," I said.

"Made with wood that my local wood yard sold . . . along with thirty other wood yards in the state! Yes, the wood could have come from the Bronx, but the kidnapper could have got it from any one of the other thirty yards!"

"The police never said that in court," I said. "But then that floorboard from your attic was the clincher."

He looked me in the face for the first time. His eyes were shadowed with rings as blue as wood smoke. "Mr Elliot," he said quietly, "why would I use a piece of wood from my attic? Why would I rip up a floorboard when I could have simply bought another piece of wood?"

"So who made that rung 16?" I asked.

"Did you know that my wife lived in the house while the police searched it for clues? But she was so disturbed she moved out. It was *after* she moved out that they say they found that floorboard."

"You're saying the police ripped up the floorboard and made that rung? The police framed you?" I asked. "Can you prove that?"

"No. And I can't disprove it either," he said. "But I will tell you one thing: that ladder was very badly made. Look at how it cracked when the kidnapper climbed down it."

"So?"

"So, you are forgetting I am a trained carpenter. I could

not make a bad ladder if I tried." He had a point – another one of those points the jury ignored.

"There was a phone number scribbled on a wall in a cupboard," I reminded him. "It was the phone number of Condon, the go-between."

He spread those hands wide and helpless again. "Why would I write that number in a cupboard? I have never had a phone in the house! What use is it written there? I don't know who wrote it. All I do know is it wasn't me."

"OK, Mr Hauptmann, let's look at the ransom notes. The writer couldn't spell. When the police asked you to write the messages you made the same spelling mistakes," I told him.

"Oh, no, Mr Elliot. The police did not ask me to *write* the messages, they asked me to *copy* them. Complete with the spelling mistakes."

"They never said that in court either," I said, shaking my head.

"Like they never said that Condon heard voices in the background when he phoned the kidnapper. Those voices were speaking in Italian," Hauptmann said.

"Italian? As in Mafia?" I said. "You think this was a Mafia kidnapping?"

The man shook his head slowly. "I don't know. All I know is that I didn't do it."

"The rest of the world seems to disagree, Mr Hauptmann," I said.

"So you won't help me?"

I thought about it for a while. "The state governor tried to sack the man who was your prosecutor. The press say the governor is backing an appeal. I'll talk to him and see what he has to say."

I stood up. Hauptmann stretched out a hand. A large hand, a rough hand. The hand of a carpenter for sure. The hand of a killer? Who knows?

"Hauptmann will die," Governor Hoffman told me. "The American people were horrified by the death of little Buster. They can't believe an American would do such a thing to the son of their hero."

"But a German . . ." I said, following his line of thought. "They'd rather believe a foreigner could do it?"

He nodded. "Hauptmann will die because the people want someone to blame. I agree with you, all the evidence is very, very suspect. I wouldn't be surprised if the police did manufacture some of it, just as you say. After all, the whole world has told our police they're the greatest detectives in the world to crack this case. They like that. They're not going to admit they're a bunch of crooks, are they? No, Mr Elliot, you should know – a detective's job is to come up with answers. And sometimes detectives come up with answers that people want, not the answers that are the truth. I've done my best to get Hauptmann a fair hearing, and you've done your best, Mr Elliot. But sometimes that's not good enough."

"So who really killed Buster Lindbergh?" I asked him.

"We don't know," he said quietly. "And I have a feeling we never will."

31

*F*ACT FILE

The Lindbergh kidnapping – FACT FILE

1. Bruno Hauptmann was unlucky. The law was out to make sure he paid for the kidnapping, even if he didn't do it. The child was snatched from the Lindberghs' home in the state of New Jersey. In New Jersey a kidnapper could only be executed if the victim died *while a robbery was being committed*. No one knew when Buster died, so Hauptmann should not have been executed. The prosecutor told the jury Buster had *probably* died in the nursery or when the ladder snapped. They believed him.

2. After the Lindbergh kidnapping the laws were changed to make punishment easier. Anyone committing a kidnap could be executed if the victim suffered any harm at all. Even sending a ransom note could cost twenty years in jail, a $5,000 fine or both.

3. Modern detection has shed new light on the case:

- Hauptmann was telling the truth when he said the money box had been damaged by damp.
- In the 1990s, handwriting experts looked

again at Hauptmann's writing and the writing on the kidnap notes. They disagreed with the 1934 expert and said the kidnap notes were almost certainly *not* written by Hauptmann.

- Fisch *did* owe Hauptmann over $7,000 and *was* involved in a lot of illegal deals. Fisch could well have "bought" the Lindbergh kidnap money that Hauptmann was storing in his attic, but he died in Germany in the year of Hauptmann's trial and so could not be found to back up the accused man's story.

- The wood technologist, Koehler, said that his method of looking at saw marks, wood grain, tree rings, knot holes and nail holes was as sure a proof as fingerprinting. In fact it isn't. This "greatest feat of scientific detection of all time" is no more accurate than handwriting tests.

4. The governor of the prison, Harold Hoffmann, interviewed Hauptmann several times in his cell and did not believe that the accused man was guilty. He tried to help the German to prove his case. Hauptmann offered to take truth drugs and lie-detector tests to prove his innocence, but the police refused. Hauptmann was executed in 1935.

5. There is a strange theory that little Buster never died at all. A baby's skeleton was

found near an orphanage. It could not be identified, though Buster's nurse said she recognized the rotting shirt in which the baby was wrapped. Was the body in fact one of the orphans? And was Buster actually kidnapped by the Mafia as some people suspected? A baby of the right age was handed by gangsters to a family to raise as their own son. (With the huge hunt that went on for the baby, the kidnappers may have decided it was too risky to try to 'cash in' on him, and they didn't want to kill him.) Before the mother died she told the boy that she believed he was Charles Lindbergh's son. The boy grew up to be Harold Olson. Photographs show that Buster Lindbergh had a scar on his chin and Harold Olson had a scar in exactly the same place.

THE CASE OF THE POISONED PIGS

Think of detectives and you usually think of the police. But some of the greatest puzzles have been solved by the people who help the police – the scientists.

Victoria State, Australia, February 1940

"Somebody poisoned my pig!" the woman said, and she hit the top of the police station counter with a large fist. It was a strong fist. Everything about the middle-aged woman was strong – including her smell, Sergeant Sharp thought. He couldn't help wrinkling his nose a little as he pulled out a pencil.

"Name, madam?" he asked, opening the report book to note the details.

"Blenkinsop. Alicia Blenkinsop," the woman said, pulling her overall round her large chest. Her face was as brown and tough as boot leather. Her eyes were pale blue marbles, sunken and small in folds of fat.

"Address, Mrs Blenkinsop?"

"Yarra Glen Model Pig Farm."

"And what seems to be the problem?" the policeman asked as he leaned back out of the way of the woman's pig-swill scent. It was hot in this small station and the summer air was suffocating enough. The young sergeant ran a finger under his collar and wished he could get a job in one of those patrol cars. That was the life!

Instead he was stuck in here with this woman talking to him. No, not talking – shouting. "I just *told* you, somebody poisoned my *pig*! Not an ordinary pig, a valuable *prize* pig!" Every time she said the letter "p" she sprayed Doug Sharp's face with spittle. He leaned back further. "A *pedigree* pig!" she finished.

"You sure it's poison? Couldn't have been natural causes?" he asked. It wasn't often he had the chance to play detective and he was going to make the most of it.

"Sergeant," she said, "I've worked with pigs for twenty years . . ."

And never had a bath in all that time, he thought.

"Twenty years. And I know a poisoned pig when I see one! It was lying on its back, legs in the air and belly swollen like it had swallowed a football. *Poison!*" she said, spraying the policeman again. "Poison by persons unknown." She leaned forward and finished dramatically, "Murder!"

Sergeant Sharp used his pencil to scratch his neck. "I'm not sure the death of a pig —"

"A *prize* pig!" she reminded him.

"A *prize* pig . . . I'm not sure that is classed as homicide. Maybe you should talk to the animal cruelty people. Or a vet."

"Maybe it's not homicide. Maybe it's pigicide, whatever. It was a *crime*."

"Have you any idea when the crime was committed?" the policeman asked.

"Last night," Mrs Blenkinsop said quickly. "I was lying in bed, windows open 'cos of the heat, and I heard a car coming down the track. Heard it stop near the pigsties then move off again, fast."

"What time?"

"Didn't notice. Didn't think it was important at the time," the woman shrugged.

"I see," Doug Sharp nodded. If he was going to play detective then he knew he had to work out something called "motive". "Any idea why someone might want to kill your pig?"

Mrs Blenkinsop's little blue eyes popped. She leaned forward and brought her face close to the young sergeant. "Nazis!" she hissed. "Spies!"

The policeman's mouth dropped open. "Nazi spies killed your pig, Mrs Blenkinsop? Why would they want to do that?"

"We're at war, aren't we?" she said as if that was enough answer.

"Yes, but —"

"And every pound of pig meat is part of the war effort, isn't it? 'Specially prize breeding pigs. It's called sabotage," she said. "So you get yourself out to Yarra Glen and investigate. OK?"

"Er . . . yes, Mrs Blenkinsop," Doug Sharp said.

After the woman left the policeman opened all the doors and windows to freshen the air, then put his head around the door of Detective Inspector Drysdale's office. "Murder case, sir," he said.

"Murder?" the detective said, raising a lazy eyebrow.

"Seems we have some Nazi spies trying to ruin the country by poisoning our pigs."

Drysdale's interested eyebrow dropped. "Ah, yeah. Lot of them about."

"Seriously, sir. Who do I see about a pig-poisoning case?"

The inspector pulled a blue-backed book from a drawer and ran a finger down the list of names and phone numbers. "Here's the guy: Charles Taylor, Victoria's Public Analyst. Knows more about poisons than anyone in Australia."

"Yes, sir," the sergeant said, taking the slip of paper with the telephone number.

"Oh, but Sharp . . ."

"Yes, sir?"

"If he offers you a cup of tea, don't drink it."

"Very funny, sir."

"And Sharp!"

"Yes, sir?"

"Are you responsible for that disgusting smell?"

The sergeant turned red to the roots of his sun-bleached hair. "Sorry, sir," he muttered as he backed out of the door.

It took Sergeant Sharp a long time to persuade Charles Taylor to accompany him to Yarra Glen. "I'm extremely busy," the man insisted.

"But they're pedigree pigs, Mr Taylor. Important to the war effort."

There was a long silence on the other end of the phone, then a sigh. "Very well. I'll meet you at Yarra Glen tomorrow morning."

The next morning it seemed that word had got around the small farms in the area. Every farmer for ten miles around had turned up with his family to see the famous Mr Charles Taylor at work. Mrs Blenkinsop stood proudly in her back yard, telling her visitors about the spies who came in the night. The sun burned on the baked soil and made the smell of the dead pig worse than ever.

Sergeant Sharp arrived first. Mrs Blenkinsop marched up to him. "Another one last night!" she said. "I'll be ruined at this rate."

"Another one?" Doug asked, then wished he hadn't. He

groped for a handkerchief to mop the spray he knew was coming.

"Porker!" she said. "Pedigree prize porker. Want to see it?"

Doug Sharp didn't want to see it and was glad when the sound of a car engine announced the arrival of Charles Taylor.

The group in the back yard fell silent and waited for the words of wisdom from the great man.

He stood in the yard and looked around slowly, a wide-brimmed hat shading his sharp eyes. After two minutes he stepped across to the sergeant and shook hands. "Morning," he said shortly.

"Good morning, sir. Would you like to see the pig? Another one died this morning."

"Hmm," Taylor said and gave the dead pig a quick glance. "Let's look at the layout first, shall we?"

"The layout?" Doug Sharp asked.

"That's right. Ever want to be a detective, Sergeant?" the scientist asked.

"Why, yes, sir!" the young man replied eagerly.

"Then start by looking at the scene of the crime," Charles Taylor advised. In a heat that made the distant mountains shimmer the poisons expert was as cool as the Tasman Sea. "Why do you think the pig pens were built just there?" he asked.

"Would it be the trees?" the young sergeant guessed.

Taylor nodded. "Good. These ironbark gums are the tallest trees for quite a distance. The pens were built in the shade of the trees. Let's see if there's anything in the soil that could harm the animals, shall we?"

As the silent crowd looked on, the scientist knelt and

scooped up a handful of soil from inside the pen. Even the pigs stopped eating to watch as he rubbed it between his fingers and sniffed carefully. "Healthy enough soil, pure water. You can tell by the healthy trees that are growing here," he said. Suddenly something caught his eye: a bright ball of rainbow fluff. He swooped to pick it up and slipped it into his pocket before the watchers could make out quite what it was.

He raised a lazy hand and pointed to a small mound a hundred metres or so from the pig pens. "Now, those trees over there don't look so healthy, do they?"

"No, sir," Sergeant Sharp agreed, looking at the scrawny, dwarfed plants covering the low hill.

"Let's have a look at that hill, shall we?" Taylor said and set off without waiting for an answer. Rosella parrots rose in a screeching, brilliant cloud as the men approached the mound and Charles Taylor crouched to feel the soil. "Sandy soil. And look at this," he said, holding out a handful. "See those crystals? That's the sort of gritty stuff those parrots need in their diet. Helps them to make the eggshells in their bodies. I think a sample of that will be interesting," and he scooped a small amount into his pocket.

Mrs Blenkinsop was scowling by the time he returned to her back yard. "Ain't you going to look at my poor pig?" she asked.

"I don't think so," the scientist said.

"It's *dead*!" the woman wailed. "Ain't you going to examine the *corpse*?"

"No. I can see that it's dead, and I will try to ascertain the cause," Taylor promised.

"By looking at a hill a hundred yards away?" she

screeched in disbelief. "The pigs don't eat over there. They've been poisoned in their pens by Nazi spies!"

Charles Taylor gave the woman a polite smile, raised his hat and said, "Good day, Mrs Blenkinsop. Sergeant Sharp here will be in touch."

A group of farmers were left shaking their heads as the scientist climbed into his car and drove the forty kilometres back to Melbourne.

As the day cooled into evening Doug Sharp received a message from Charles Taylor – an invitation to visit him at his laboratory in the city. The policeman arrived at eight and the scientist showed him into the room. The chemical smells were almost as disgusting as Mrs Blenkinsop's dead pig.

"Well, Sergeant, have you solved the case yet?" Taylor asked, and his eyes sparkled behind the wire-rimmed glasses.

"No . . . have you?" the policeman asked.

"If I give you all of the evidence that I have, perhaps you can crack the curious case of the poisoned pigs. Sounds like something Sherlock Holmes would be interested in," the older man smiled. He took the policeman across to a work bench and showed him two small samples of dark crystals. "These crystals are from the soil we found by the stunted trees," he explained. "Put some into this liquid for me, will you?"

Sergeant Sharp took a small spoon and carefully scooped some crystals into a test-tube full of a clear liquid. The liquid turned bright orange. "Now, Sergeant, that only happens if the crystals are of a substance called stibnite. It's usually buried deep underground, but it can

be brought to the surface during mining work. That small mound was waste from a long-gone mine. Now try this other sample of crystals."

The policeman took a second sample and tipped the crystals into a fresh tube of liquid. The liquid turned bright orange again. "More stibnite?" he asked.

"Exactly. But this second sample was from the object I picked up inside the pig pen."

"Yeah!" Doug Sharp said. "What exactly was that?"

The professor uncovered a small bundle of feathers on the end of the bench. "A Rosella parrot. Those crystals came from its stomach. Now, you have all the facts . . . solve the case."

The policeman sat on a laboratory stool and stared at the two orange test-tubes. "Is stibnite poisonous?" he asked suddenly.

"Very," the scientist nodded.

Doug Sharp took a deep breath and began to untangle the problem. "The old mine workings left the ground poisoned, so trees wouldn't grow properly. That's why

Mrs Blenkinsop chose the ironbark gum trees for her pig shade. And that's why the parrots chose the same trees to nest in."

"Good," Charles Taylor said. "We'll make a detective out of you yet."

"The parrots flew across to the poisoned ground and got a gut full of stibnite. They flew back to the ironbark gum trees to nest, died of stibnite poisoning and fell into the pig pens. The pigs ate the bodies of the parrots and died too!"

"Brilliant!" the scientist laughed and clapped his hands softly. "You should be pleased with yourself, Sergeant!"

"Yeah. I just wish they'd been kookaburras, a lyre bird or even a frogmouth – anything but a pigeon or a parrot."

"Why is that, Sergeant?"

"Oh, Mrs Blenkinsop has a little trouble with the letter 'p'," he said.

"Parrots? Perishing parrots poisoned my prize pedigree pigs!" Mrs Blenkinsop exploded.

Sergeant Doug Sharp wiped his face with a handkerchief. "I was afraid you'd say that," he muttered.

The Yarra Glen poisoning case was taken very seriously at the time. The Prime Minister of Victoria State took a personal interest and was as worried as the pig farmer that the pigs might be the victims of Nazi saboteurs. He used his power to order Charles Anthony Taylor of Melbourne University to assist the police. Taylor was known as "The Cat" because of his cunning brain and because of his initials, and he solved many cases that puzzled the police.

FACT FILE

Detectives and poison – FACT FILE

1. Experts in the study of poisons are known as toxicologists. The toxicologist's job is to separate a poison from the victim's stomach or blood and to say what type of poison it is. Modern toxicology is so sophisticated that even tiny amounts of poison can be detected. The detective's job is to find where the poisoner got the poison from and to prove that he gave it to the victim. The chance of a poisoner succeeding today is not as great as it used to be.

2. Detectives are trained to examine the scene of a sudden death very carefully for poison. Medicines found near the victim are labelled and sent for testing by toxicologists. Cups, bottles or glasses are drained and their contents tested, and detectives note any dangerous substances in an unusual place – car anti-freeze in the kitchen or weed-killer in the bedroom, say. They may also look at tea, coffee or sugar jars and smell them for anything unusual. They are, of course, told never to try tasting them!

3. Poisoning has always been considered a

45

particularly vicious way to kill somebody. The poisoner usually has to be in close contact with the victim if they are to give them the poison. That often means it is a wife, husband, relative or close friend. For this reason the chances of detecting a poisoner are usually greater. A famous case in Tudor England concerned Alice Arden, who was convicted of poisoning her husband in 1551. Killing someone so close to you was believed to be nastier than, say, a robber killing an unknown victim, so the punishment was much nastier than usual. Alice Arden was sentenced to be burned alive.

4. Other unpopular poisoners had their executions recorded by poets. These people wrote verses about the killer which usually damned him, gloated over his death and said it was a warning to others. They were printed and sold for a penny. A typical example was *The Execution of Alice Holt*:

A dreadful case of poison, such as we seldom hear,
Committed was at Stockport, in the county of Cheshire.
Where a mother named Mary Bailey, they did so cruelly slaughter,
By poison administered all in her beer, by her own daughter.

The daughter insured the life of her
    mother, for £26 at her death,
Then she and the man she lived with
    determined to take away her breath.
She made a plan to murder her, as we now
    see so clear,
To put a quantity of arsenic into her poor
    mother's beer.

But there's no doubt the base wretch did
    her poor mother slay,
For which on Chester scaffold her life did
    forfeit pay.
So all young women a warning take, by
    this poor wretch you see,
A-hanging for her mother's sake on
    Chester's fatal tree.

The poisoning was a nasty crime . . . and that
sort of verse was a bit of a crime against the
art of poetry!

5. The poison arsenic was invented by an
Arab chemist. It was used in killing flies and
in making beauty treatments, so it was
widely available. A certain amount of
arsenic is naturally present in the human
body and in certain foods we eat and is
harmless in small quantities. Some people
used to eat small quantities of the poison as a
tonic to make them feel fit! But arsenic is
poisonous in doses of more than 65mg. Many

famous poisoners used arsenic because it had little taste and could be mixed with food. Then, when the victim began to die, their doctor would often believe they had a natural stomach illness, often called 'gastric fever'.

The disadvantage of using arsenic as a poison was that victims would have traces of arsenic in their hair, nails or bones long after they had been buried. Some poisoners were detected in this way years after they thought they had "got away with murder". That's what happened in a famous English case.

Poisoning used to be a popular way of getting rid of an unwanted person because the killer could be many miles away by the time his victim died. In many cases doctors would conclude that the victim had died of natural causes. Some poisoners saw their victims buried and would have got away with their crime if they hadn't become over-confident and tried to do it again.

Hay-on-Wye, England, 1922

"Twenty packets of arsenic, please," the small man ordered. He looked as if he was used to giving orders, a military man with a back as stiff and straight as his walking cane and a moustache that bristled like the back of an angry cat.

"You'll have to sign the poisons book, Major," Edward Mann the chemist said as he reached for the arsenic jar and began to measure out the white powder.

"Of course, of course!" Major Armstrong barked.

The chemist squinted carefully at the scales as he let the powder drop into the brass pan. "More than 65 milligrams can kill a man," he warned. He tipped the measured powder on to a small square of paper and folded it carefully, then began to measure out the second portion. "And you don't have to swallow it," he went on. "You can poison yourself by breathing in the dust."

"Don't worry," Major Armstrong said. "I place it in a squirt gun with a pointed nozzle. I then insert the nozzle into the ground at the root of the dandelion and squirt. Kills the dandelion but not the grass around it. I hate dandelions. Hate them, hate them!" he said, and his blue eyes glittered behind his gold-rimmed glasses.

Edward Mann folded the second packet and carried on

working while he talked slowly to his customer. "Sickness and diarrhoea," he said, "they're the first signs of arsenic poisoning. So if you feel the first sign of sickness, see your doctor."

"Fit as a flea! Fit as a flea!" The major gave a barking laugh but his eyes never left the packets of deadly powder as they piled up on the chemist's workbench.

"There you are!" Edward Mann said finally. "Twenty packets of arsenic."

The small major gave a satisfied twist to the end of his moustache. "Twenty dead dandelions," he said grimly. He signed the poison register and picked up the brown-paper bag, then, with a "Good day to you, Mr Mann," he raised his hat politely and marched out of the chemist's shop.

"Funny chap, that Major Armstrong," Edward Mann said that evening as he ate supper with his daughter Eunice and her husband Arthur Martin. "His office is across the road from yours, isn't it, Arthur?"

Arthur had a long, sad face like an overworked horse. "It is. And I wish it wasn't. We're the only two solicitors in town and there's more than enough work for both of us, yet he seems to see me as some kind of rival." The young man leaned forward and said quietly, "He watches me."

"You never said, Arthur!" Eunice put in. She had a plump and worried face. Her eyes grew wide with wonder.

"Sometimes I look up from my desk and I see him standing at the window of his office, staring."

"Staring?"

"Staring straight at me," Arthur said.

"Ooh, Arthur! And he has those creepy pale blue eyes, doesn't he?"

"He does," Arthur nodded his cart-horse head. "But why do you say he's a funny chap, Dad?" the young solicitor asked his father-in-law.

"Because he has an obsession about dandelions. Says he hates them," Edward Mann explained.

"Ooh! Yes, he would," Eunice nodded and her plump chin trembled a little. "He lives in that huge house at the end of the town. 'Mayfield' it's called. Bea-oooo-tiful lawns. Seems to be a hobby with him."

"Hobby!" her father snorted. "More like an obsession. Still, he must be doing well from that solicitor business," he went on, nudging Arthur in the ribs with an elbow. "You'll be buying a big house for Eunice when you're that rich, I expect."

Arthur shook his long, worried head. "I don't make that much money," he said, "and the major seems to have even fewer clients than I do."

"So where does he get his money from?" Edward Mann asked.

"His wife – his *late* wife, I should say," Eunice explained. Poor woman died last February. Changed her will just before she died. Left all her money to the major." She leaned forward over the tea table and said quietly, "He *earned* her money, by all accounts."

"How do you mean, my dear?" her husband asked.

"She gave him a terrible life. *Terrible*. She wouldn't let him smoke or drink in the house. And when he was up at the tennis club she'd show him up something rotten. More than once she came and dragged him off the tennis court if he was two minutes late for dinner!"

Edward Mann blinked. In that blink he saw the major's pale blue eyes glittering behind gold-rimmed glasses. He saw arsenic powder . . . and he saw a dead woman. He blinked again and tried to forget the disturbing picture. Luckily for Eunice and Arthur, he didn't forget it entirely.

Two weeks later Arthur fell ill.

Eunice chewed the corner of a handkerchief as she tried to tell her father why he wouldn't be joining them for supper that night. "The doctor gave him bicarbonate of soda but it hasn't settled him. He's being terribly sick."

Edward Mann frowned. "What has he been eating?" he asked.

"Nothing that I haven't eaten too," she sniffed. Suddenly her eyes began to glisten with tears. "You're not saying my cooking has made him ill?" she said.

He wrapped an arm around her shoulder. "No, no. But he must sometimes eat outside the house. Let's ask him, shall we?"

She sniffed and nodded. The chemist and his daughter climbed the dark stairway to the small bedroom. Arthur's bed was a tangled mess and the young solicitor was thrashing about wildly, groaning and clutching his stomach. The chemist looked into the sick bowl by the bedside. "Here, Father, I'll take that away," Eunice said, reaching for the bowl.

"Scones!" her husband cried suddenly.

"Scones? You want me to cook you some scones?" Eunice asked.

"Scones. Went to tea . . . with Major Armstrong . . . discussing a case . . . gave me a scone . . . strange!" Arthur gasped.

"That was nice of him," Eunice said, adding quietly to her father, "He's been having these strange hallucinations."

Edward Mann leaned forward. "What was strange about the scone, Arthur?" he asked carefully.

"He handed me the scone . . . he didn't pass the plate . . . 'Excuse my fingers,' he said. . . handed me the scone."

"I see," the chemist breathed. "He wanted you to have that particular scone, did he?"

Arthur made a huge effort, turned his head and looked into the eyes of his father-in-law. "Poison!" he managed to say.

Eunice gave a small gasp. "Should we send him to the hospital?" she asked.

"No. We have everything we need in the shop downstairs," he said briskly. "We'll test for the poison and give him the right cure much quicker than any hospital could. Fetch Arthur's bowl," he ordered. "Just as well you didn't throw it away."

The chemist bounded down the stairs and Eunice scrambled after him. He unlocked the door into his workshop and began assembling the apparatus he would need. He spoke quickly. "Eunice, you used to help me in the shop when you were younger. I'll need your help now."

"Yes, Father. What do you want me to do?"

"Take some of the contents of the bowl and pour it through a funnel into a test-tube," he ordered while he selected a bottle of pale golden liquid and lit a gas burner under a glass jar.

"But you can't test for every poison," Eunice said as she began the unpleasant task of filling the test-tube.

"You're right. I'll test for just one. If that is negative we'll send for the ambulance," he said. "Now, add half of the contents of the test-tube to the liquid in this jar."

"What is it?"

"Hydrochloric acid," he said. "Hurry, girl!"

He didn't usually speak to her so sharply. She tipped some of her test-tube contents into the boiling acid and stepped back. Her father stirred it with a glass rod, then took it away from the heat. Then he took a thin strip of copper from his cupboard and dipped it into the mixture in the jar. He removed it ten seconds later. It was covered with a dull, grey coating.

"This is called Reinsch's test," he explained. "And that grey coating proves that your husband has swallowed arsenic."

The police inspector sat in the armchair and looked at the three worried people. "Yes, Mr Mann, our tests confirm that your son-in-law has swallowed arsenic. Indeed he is lucky to be alive. Your prompt action probably saved him."

Eunice squeezed her father's hand and smiled faintly at her husband.

"You'll arrest Major Armstrong, then?" she said.

Inspector Harris shook his head. "Madam, we cannot go around arresting respectable citizens like the major without evidence."

The chemist rose to his feet, agitated. "He gave my son-in-law the poisoned scone . . ."

"You say he gave the young gentleman a scone, but can you prove that? Then, can you prove that scone was poisoned?"

"No, but . . . I can prove that he bought arsenic from my shop."

"And how many other people have bought arsenic from how many other shops in this country?" the policeman asked. Edward Mann stayed silent. "You see, sir, we have no link between the arsenic the major bought and the arsenic found in your son-in-law's stomach. And then the court would expect you to establish a motive. Why would the major want to kill Mr Martin?"

"We are in dispute over a legal matter between one of his clients and one of mine," Arthur Martin said quickly.

"Hardly a reason to kill you. And you did stay on friendly terms. Why, he even invited you to tea!" the policeman pointed out.

"And what about the chocolates?" Eunice put in.

"Ah, the chocolates," Inspector Harris said. "You received a gift of chocolates in the post. The sender did not enclose his or her name. You don't eat chocolates so you placed them on the dinner table for guests. Your guests were very sick afterwards. Well, we shall take the remaining chocolates away for examination, but even if they do contain arsenic you cannot prove they were sent by the major."

The chemist spoke up. "What you need is a clear link with Major Armstrong. You need a strong reason for the major to poison someone, and a body – a dead body – full of arsenic," he concluded.

"Precisely, sir."

"Then I think I can tell you exactly where you'll find such a body," the chemist said.

Arthur Martin hung up the telephone earpiece with

difficulty. His hand was trembling. He was paler than he had been when he was suffering from poisoning.

"It was Major Armstrong, wasn't it?" Eunice asked.

"He wants me to come to tea," her husband said.

"You didn't accept?" she gasped.

"He said we have a case to discuss. Would I come to tea at his house. That's the third time this week he's invited me." The young solicitor's haunted eyes met his wife's. "I'm running out of excuses to refuse, Eunice! And he's still watching me. Everywhere I go he is watching me. I imagine arsenic in everything I eat. My nerves can't stand the strain much longer!" he moaned.

Edward Mann stepped through the doorway from his shop and walked across to where his son-in-law sat trembling by the telephone. "Not much longer now, Arthur. The police will dig up the body tonight. I will be there as a witness."

"When will they know the results?" Eunice asked.

"I think you will find they know as soon as they open the coffin," the chemist assured her.

Inspector Harris introduced the men quickly. "Mr Mann, this is Sir Bernard Spillsbury, England's leading expert on post-mortem examinations."

The chemist shook his hand but said nothing. He simply turned to watch the four policemen in shirt-sleeves as they took turns to dig through the damp soil of the grave.

Anyone walking past the churchyard would have been horrified at the sight of the men gathered round the grave like bodysnatchers of old. Only three lanterns lit their work. They had chosen to dig at night rather than let the whole town know their business.

Finally the coffin was hauled to the surface. Inspector Harris brushed loose soil from the name plate. "Mrs Jane Armstrong," he read. "Yes, this is the major's wife. Let's have a quick look before we take her to your laboratory, Sir Bernard."

The policeman began to unscrew the coffin lid very carefully. Finally the men stepped forward with a lantern and looked in. "Died last February?" Sir Bernard asked.

"That's correct," the inspector said.

"Then her body is beautifully preserved. Too well preserved. Arsenic poisoning does that to a body." The expert looked at the chemist and said, "You will be relieved to hear, sir, that Major Armstrong has a case to answer. A case of murder."

FACT FILE

Serial poisoners – FACT FILE

1. Mrs Armstrong's body was indeed full of arsenic poison. The major was arrested and the full horror of his crimes became clear. He had altered his wife's will so that he gained her considerable fortune when she died. His business was doing badly at the time and he needed the money. The local doctor had concluded that Mrs Armstrong had died naturally and she was buried. The major had got away with murder . . . so he tried again. He argued with a businessman called Davies, invited him to tea and poisoned him. Davies died and his doctor found the cause of death to be appendicitis. Major Armstrong had got away with murder again! When he wanted rid of Arthur Martin, the only competition in Hay town, he sent poisoned chocolates. They didn't work, but the poisoned scone very nearly did. Only the experienced eye of young Martin's father-in-law, the chemist, recognized the effects of arsenic. Major Armstrong was executed and Martin was saved. He and the dandelions lived to fight another year!

2. The police do sometimes catch poisoners without the help of local chemists. Samuel Doss died in Tulsa, Oklahoma, in 1954 after eating a plate of prunes. On examining his body the police doctor found enough poison in his stomach to kill ten men. Mrs Doss was shocked. "How on earth did that happen?" she wanted to know. The police suggested that perhaps she had slipped the poison into the prunes. "My conscience is clear," she said. Then they did a little digging into her past and found that *four* husbands before Doss had all died with stomach pains, as well as her mother, two sisters and three other children! She was another poisoner who just kept on poisoning until she was caught. Many famous poisoners seem to keep on poisoning people even when they have no need to.

3. A doctor called Palmer murdered a friend called Cook in 1855. The examination of Cook's body was a joke! Palmer, being a friend of the dead man as well as a doctor, was allowed to be present at the examination. Cook's stomach was full of strychnine poison but as it was lifted from the body, Palmer gave the surgeon a push and the contents spilled on to the floor! Cook was the last of a long line of Palmer's victims; later investigation showed he was the fourteenth! The doctor might have escaped again but at Cook's examination he

tried to bribe the magistrate and the police at last became suspicious. He was executed.

4. Another deadly doctor was Neill Cream. He was practising in America when he poisoned one of his patients. Instead of being executed he was sentenced to prison and released in less than ten years. He decided to continue his criminal habit in England. In 1892 he began poisoning women. After four deaths he seemed somehow disappointed that the police were nowhere near catching him. He went to New Scotland Yard and said he was being followed by villains, and asked for a detective to accompany him. The more friendly the detective became, the more Cream gave himself away. But the final proof came from a young woman who did *not* die from Cream's poison tablets – she'd thrown them in the Thames and lived. Her evidence led to his execution.

5. Clever poisoners could beat the Reinsch test for arsenic. A doctor called Smethurst married an older woman in 1859 and began to poison her with arsenic so that he could inherit her money. The woman's own doctor, Doctor Bird, suspected arsenic poisoning and the police arrested Doctor Smethurst for attempted murder. There was no proof at that stage so the magistrate released Smethurst, giving him the chance to

finish the job of poisoning his wife! He cleverly disguised the arsenic by adding chlorate of potash to it and this defeated the Reinsch test. There was a lot of arsenic in the poor woman's body but the potash trick confused the case and Smethurst was set free.

THE CAT BURGLAR

A detective's work is not always as exciting and interesting as it is made to appear in books, films or television. One of a detective's main areas of work is 'surveillance' – watching a criminal or a place where you believe a crime might be committed. This is often a long, boring and uncomfortable task. When it succeeds, of course, the effort seems worthwhile.

London, 1924

When I was a young copper I made a big mistake. I was lucky. I learned from my mistake. I never made that mistake again and I became a better policeman as a result. Let me tell you about it.

I'd just been selected to join London's Flying Squad – at least that's what the newspapers called our section. Our correct title was Mobile Patrol Squad, but no one ever called us that.

I was thrilled! The squad was made up of the best detectives in the fastest cars. They didn't just examine crimes and try to catch the criminals, they went out and stopped crime before it happened. They kept a secret watch on known criminals, and even drank with them in local pubs – in disguise, of course.

After spending two years based at an ordinary police station in the East End of London, I was itching for the sort of excitement the Flying Squad seemed to offer: car chases with desperate criminals, arresting dangerous and violent men and being at the scene of big crimes when they happened.

I was disappointed, of course. The Flying Squad got results from hard work, long hours and a lot of boring routine.

I was almost ready to pack it in and go back to my old job when I was given an "observation" job.

The chief inspector spoke to a dozen of the squad on a Thursday morning in October. "There are some areas of London that are so rich they attract a thief like jam attracts a wasp. Mayfair is one, St James's another."

We knew that, of course. Why was he telling us? I shifted in my seat and waited for him to get to the point. "There is some evidence that many of the burglaries in Mayfair are being carried out by the same man. The same method is used each time, and it's very successful. In the past five weeks we reckon he's got away with £30,000-worth of cash and jewellery."

£30,000! That was an absolute fortune in 1924, you have to remember. The rest of the detectives sat up too. "How does he do it?" Bob Fabian asked quickly.

Bob was sharp. He'd joined the squad at the same time as me but he was much brighter. The chief inspector gave a thin smile. "I wish we knew. Most of the robberies are from hotel bedrooms. When the residents go down to dinner in the evening, our friend comes in through the window and leaves the same way."

There seemed to be a dozen questions at once.

"He must have a ladder," one detective chipped in. "And you can't walk through the London streets with a ladder without being stopped by a policeman on the beat, can you?"

"He seems to go over the roofs and climb *without* a ladder," the chief inspector said.

"More like a cat," someone joked. We laughed, but the name stuck. From then on he was nicknamed the Cat Burglar.

"But Mayfair's a wealthy area," Bob argued. "Surely a burglar couldn't wander along without being noticed?"

"Maybe he's disguised," I guessed.

Some of the others shook their heads as if it were a stupid idea and I blushed and wished I hadn't spoken. Bob Fabian came to my rescue. He took me seriously. "He *must* be," he agreed. "What disguise could he use that would let him walk through Mayfair without being stopped and questioned?"

The chief inspector shrugged. "If we knew that, then we'd probably catch him."

"What are we going to do about him?" someone asked.

"We're going to keep a watch on all the big hotels. We'll hide and look out for anything suspicious."

I groaned softly to myself. I'd joined the Flying Squad looking for excitement. Instead I was going to spend hour after hour, night after night, sitting in the cold and dark looking for an invisible man.

"You will work in pairs," the chief inspector was saying. "We'll only cover half as many hotels that way, but at least you'll keep each other awake. And you'll be in a stronger position to make an arrest. If this man's a climber then you can bet he'll be strong as an ox. It might well take two of you to hold him!"

That was a worry. But the good news was that I was paired with Bob Fabian.

We were given the famous Ritz Hotel to watch. We sat among the dustbins in the dark back yard. The sour smell of stale food mixed with the mouth-watering scents from the hotel kitchens.

Bob kept me cheerful but he couldn't take away the

cold and the stiffness. By the time we went home in the morning I was ready to resign. That second night I began to wish that the Cat Burglar would appear. I didn't want someone to be robbed, you understand; I just wanted the excitement of the chase and the thrill of the arrest.

At the same time I was sure we were like cats sitting waiting at an empty mousehole. I was bored. But Bob Fabian was a better detective. He had endless patience. Even while he was chatting his eyes never stopped scanning the curtained windows and the darkened gardens below them. Suddenly he stopped in the middle of a sentence and gripped my arm.

His other hand was pointing towards the back of the houses in Arlington Street. I screwed up my eyes and saw a shadow moving within the shadows. Someone was entering the back gate.

The figure was moving too carefully to be the owner of the house. Bob and I rose to our feet. I forgot about my stiffness and the cold. I forgot about resigning. This was the chase. This was what I'd joined the Flying Squad for.

We followed as quietly and quickly as we could. We entered the garden just in time to see the man climb a high fence and disappear over the far side. When I reached it I realized there was no way I could ever climb it! The man wasn't a cat – he climbed more like a spider!

"We've lost him!" I groaned.

Bob nodded. "At least we know his disguise," he said quietly.

"We do?"

"Yes. Didn't you see the glint of a diamond button on the front of a white shirt?" he asked.

"Ah . . . yes," I lied. I'd been too busy looking at my feet to take proper note of the man's appearance.

"He dresses like a gentleman: black suit, white starched shirt with fancy buttons. No one would ever think of stopping him in Mayfair to ask about a burglary."

"No," I agreed.

"Stay in the back street," Bob ordered. He seemed to know what to do, so I didn't mind him taking charge.

"Where are you going?" I asked quickly. I didn't fancy coming face to face with the man who could climb that fence.

"I'll warn the owners of these houses to check their valuables," he said as he hurried off down the dim lane.

I stared up at the backs of the houses. Now my tired eyes were sharp as a sparrow-hawk's. The Flying Squad cars had radios and I wished I'd had one there. If the rest of the squad could be brought in to surround the street, then we'd have caught the burglar there and then.

Instead I had to watch, helpless, as the Cat Burglar appeared on a balcony. I waited for him to drop down and hurry through the garden, out of the gate and into my waiting arms. My heart was beating so hard I could feel the blood pounding through my head. My handcuffs jangled in my trembling hands and I almost dropped them.

To my amazement he didn't climb down. Instead he threw something up to the roof, climbed up it and vanished over the rooftops. I'm ashamed to admit it, but I felt relieved I didn't have to tackle him alone.

I was even more ashamed the next morning when I found he'd escaped with over £2,000-worth of jewellery. Of course we were the centre of attention when we got back to headquarters. Bob's information about the Cat Burglar's smart clothes was vital.

"The strange thing is that he was wearing soft rubber soles on his shoes," Bob said.

"How do you know?" someone asked.

"I checked the balcony for footprints," my partner explained.

"Yes. That is strange," the chief inspector nodded.

"But why?" I had to ask. I knew I should have worked it out for myself but remember, I was still young in those days.

Bob smiled. "This man takes a lot of trouble to wear smart evening clothes. That should include smart leather shoes, otherwise he'd look odd. Smart shoes have leather soles. Yet he has crêpe rubber soles on his shoes to grip while he's climbing."

"So we're looking for a man in smart clothes with odd shoes?" I asked stupidly.

"Or we're looking for a pair of smart shoes especially made with rubber soles!" the chief inspector said excitedly.

Bob nodded. He knew that all along. I wish he'd told me instead of letting me make all the wrong guesses. No one noticed my slowness. They were as excited as the chief inspector.

"If we have to question every shoemaker in London we'll find who owns those shoes!" the chief inspector said. Another long and tiring job! How did I ever imagine the Flying Squad would be exciting?

In fact Bob Fabian had his usual luck. Don't get me wrong, Bob was a brilliant detective, but he had the greatest quality any detective could have. Luck!

We could have searched for weeks. In fact Bob came across the answer in just a day and a half.

The shoemaker had a shop in Albermarle Street. We entered and asked the usual question, "Have you made a pair of smart shoes with crêpe soles?"

We expected the usual answer, that no one ever has crêpe soles on evening shoes. But this time the old man smiled a wrinkled, puzzled smile. "Now, it's strange you should ask that. A gentleman bought a pair just a month ago."

I think I stopped breathing for half a minute while Bob Fabian asked softly, "And do you know the man's address?"

The shoemaker nodded. "Of course, sir," and he opened an old cash book. He ran his finger up the list of entries. "Yes, here it is!"

We hurried from the shop with the address copied carefully on to a piece of paper. "It was so easy!" I grinned.

Bob didn't smile. "Nothing's ever that easy," he said. "If you were as clever as this thief, would you give your correct name?"

"Why . . . no," I admitted.

"And you might not even give your right address."

My heart sank. "So that name and address is worse than useless? We've just wasted two days?"

"No, no, no!" Bob said. "The shoemaker described the man, didn't he? His height, his appearance and, most important of all, his American accent."

"That's not a lot to go on. Where do we start?"

"At this address, of course," Bob Fabian said briskly. "27 Half Moon Street."

The woman at 27 Half Moon Street lived alone. She was sixty years old and couldn't climb on top of her table never mind a roof top. And the couple at 26 and the young man at 28 were all clearly innocent. But at 29 we struck gold.

"No one of that name here," the young woman said.

"A tall man, dark hair, American accent?" Bob persisted.

Her eyes widened. "Ah! You have the number the wrong way round! Not 27, it's 72. And he's not American, he's Canadian. My cleaner works for him too. Says he's a nice quiet gentleman. Sleeps most of the day and seems to work nights."

"His name?"

She frowned. "Delaney. Yes, that's it, Robert Delaney!"

As she closed the door Bob Fabian turned to me. "This time . . . this time we have our man!"

The squad joined us and we moved in on Delaney's flat. The chief inspector gave Bob Fabian the honour of arresting him, while I had the honour of snapping the handcuffs on the Cat's Burglar's powerful wrists.

Robert Augustus Delaney went to prison for three years.

Bob Fabian went on to become one of the most brilliant detectives the Flying Squad has ever seen. I learned a lot from him in the years I worked with him.

But I'd made that stupid mistake at first. I'd believed that good detection was all about following clues and solving mysteries. That's not the *whole* truth.

Good detection is mostly about patience and hard work. Long hours of watching and waiting. Long miles of walking the streets and asking questions.

Bob knew that. I didn't. That was my mistake.

FACT FILE

The Flying Squad – FACT FILE

Sometimes police forces set up special detective squads to catch particular types of criminal. One of the most famous is the British Police Force's "Flying Squad".

1. The Flying Squad was formed in 1919. It began with just twelve detectives and two horse-drawn wagons. Now it has over 200 detectives and some of the fastest cars on Britain's roads.

2. The Flying Squad officers get a lot of valuable information by pretending to be friendly with criminals. In 1944 a new section of the Flying Squad was set up. A group of just four or five officers had to mix in the criminal "underworld", but not be seen as police officers. They had to be practically "invisible" as they gathered information. They were told to be as invisible as ghosts. They were known as "The Ghost Squad". In 1944 they made more arrests than any other Flying Squad officers.

3. The Ghost Squad made good use of informers – criminals who were paid to tell

the police who had committed certain crimes or who was planning a crime. Informers worked in secret. The criminals could kill them if they found out who was betraying them, so the Ghost Squad's informers used code names. Some curious ones included Slicer Fred, Stir-happy Lou and Bert the Lorry.

4. Londoners used rhyming slang to give the Flying Squad its nickname, The Sweeney. This is short for Sweeney Todd. Todd was a famous character in Victorian stories, a barber who murdered his customers and had them made into meat pies. A television series was made in the 1970s about the Flying Squad. It was called *The Sweeney*.

5. Working too closely with the underworld has its problems. In the 1970s some officers became too friendly with the criminals and began to take bribes. In return they let the crooks get away with some of their crimes. The Flying Squad officers were eventually caught and sent to prison.

The Flying Squad officers were not the only ones to cross the line from solving crimes to committing crimes.

THE PERFECT CRIME

The T

The T

V

ESTABLISHED 1896

Mothers Anger Over Blackmail

Monster threatens to put razor blades in Baby food

There were angry scenes today outside a leading high street supermarket where mothers had gathered to protest over the recent "baby-food blackmail" scare.

It was announced this morning that a threat to place razor blades in unspecified baby food had been

Mrs Gwen Limpstone, a mother of two, demanded to know why the store had kept the blackmail demands a secret for two weeks. She told The Times, "If I'd known there was somebody threatening to put razor blades in the food, I would have gone somewhere else. risk my child's ly angry that

The R Later

A stor when causi but w his

discovered a supermarket olice have on the may be eported ade to e Forb

CREDIT CARD

VISA

There's an old saying, "Set a thief to catch a thief." Thieves are experts in crime, so they should be able to detect the work of other criminals. But the darker side of this is "Set a law man to beat a law man" – a policeman should make an excellent criminal because he knows how the enemy works.

England, 1989

The man slipped a plastic card into the cash machine, punched in some numbers, and a few minutes later walked away with a handful of cash.

The street was quiet at that time of night. No one saw him get back into his car and drive away. No one heard him chuckle to himself, "The perfect crime!"

"It's the perfect crime," Martin Evans groaned and shook his head. He looked too young to be a policeman, but he was. He almost looked too young to be sitting in that smoky pub sipping a pint of beer.

Rod Whitchelo rested his elbows on the table and looked at the young detective. "I always thought there was such a thing as a perfect crime. I even thought of writing a book about it when I left the police force."

"You did?" Detective Constable Evans said. He enjoyed these chats with Rod Whitchelo after work each evening. Rod had a lot of experience and gave him tips on some of his cases.

"Yeah. So tell me again about this one. I might be able to use some tips," Whitchelo grinned. He was a heavy man and his strong hands gripped the beer glass.

Martin Evans sat back. "This criminal has been planning it for a long time. First he opened a bank account two years ago – so long ago that no one in the bank can remember what he looks like. Then he sent a letter to the director of a pet-food company. In the letter he said he would poison cans of dog food on supermarket shelves across the country. Once dog owners found out about it they would stop buying that dog food and the company would lose millions of pounds. All the criminal wanted was £100,000."

"Extortion. It's an easy way to make money," Rod Whitchelo commented.

"But we always catch blackmailers like that. It's like kidnappers. There's one weak spot in any plan: that's the moment when the criminal picks up the cash. We can mark the bank notes, put a tracking device in the container and surround the area with plain-clothes observers. That's why it's such a rare crime in Britain. They know they can't get away with it!" the young detective said.

"But this pet-food poisoner found a way round that?" Whitchelo said slowly.

"Yes. He asked the company to pay money into his bank account – the one he opened two years ago. He can go to any cash-dispensing machine and draw out a couple of hundred pounds every day. But there are nine hundred of his bank's cash tills around the country. He can draw money from any one of them. *Nine hundred!* He can visit one at any time. There's no chance of him getting caught."

"So the pet-food company paid?" Whitchelo asked.

"We advised them to go along with the plan while we worked on catching the man," Martin Evans said.

"What were you looking for?"

"A pattern. We wanted to see where he drew the money out. We could watch the cash machine and catch him," the young detective said. "Of course he was too clever for that. He drew the money out all over the country – Wales one day, Scotland the next. All we could do was wait for him to make a mistake."

"He sounds too clever to make a mistake," Whitchelo shrugged.

"But he has!" Martin cried, and his eyes glowed with triumph. "He got greedy! He threatened to put razor blades in baby food. Asked for another £100,000 to stop."

"That's not exactly greedy," Whitchelo argued. "Those food manufacturers make millions of pounds. And it's hardly a *mistake*."

"Oh, but it *is*!" the detective constable said. "It's one thing threatening to kill a dog. But threatening to kill babies is another matter. That brings in Scotland Yard and all the police forces in the country. Our Regional Crime Squad has been struggling to find time to investigate this case. Now we have the help of every police force in the country. We had ten officers on the dog-food case, but we'll have three thousand on the baby food."

Whitchelo sipped his beer thoughtfully. "I still don't see how that will help."

"It means Chief Superintendent Fleming of Scotland Yard can have each of those nine hundred cash tills watched by three men: one inside the bank reading the cash card number and two outside waiting to grab him. He won't get away this time!"

Chief Superintendent Fleming paced up and down the office. He was angry. "How did he know? We had three men watching each machine – three thousand men in all.

We couldn't miss him. So, what does our blackmailer do? He stops using the machines."

Detective Superintendent Leacey shuffled papers on his desk and pulled out a sheet. He ran a finger down the columns of figures. "You're right, sir. He drew money out every day for three weeks. On the three nights we watched the cash points he didn't draw one penny. He must have spotted one of our watchers."

"He shouldn't have. They're professionals," the Scotland Yard man snapped.

"Maybe he's a professional too," Leacey began to say when the phone on his desk rang. "Excuse me, sir," he said as he picked up the receiver. After a minute he put the phone down and looked up at the chief superintendent. "Well, sir, we have some good news and some bad news."

"Get on with it, Leacey," Fleming said.

"Our friend has drawn money out of a cash till in Ipswich."

The chief superintendent muttered a curse. "On the first night we stop watching the machines? That's too lucky to be coincidence; he must be getting inside information." He ran a hand through his short grey hair and began pacing again. "So what's the good news?"

"It seems the Ipswich branch is one where there are cameras in place – video cameras. We should be able to see his face."

Fleming stopped walking and gave a grim smile. "His first mistake, Leacey?"

"Could be, sir. A squad car has brought the video to our lecture room. Would you like to see it?"

"Would a drowning man like to see a lifebelt? Show me the way!"

But half an hour later Chief Superintendent Fleming's face was set in a scowl, making the deep lines on his face deeper and the pale, set lips thinner and harder. He stared at the image on the television screen. A man was collecting money from a cash point at a bank. Fleming could see he was tall and heavily built, but the man had cleverly placed a motorcycle crash helmet over his head. There was a smoked glass visor in front of his face.

"The picture's as much use as one of the Invisible Man," the detective from Scotland Yard said. "He knows every trick we have up our sleeves. He knew *when* we were watching and now he knows *how* we're watching."

"So what do we do, sir?" Leacey asked.

Fleming looked at him tiredly. "We give up, Leacey. We give up."

* * *

"We've given up," young Martin Evans said in the pub.

Rod Whitchelo looked into his beer and watched the bubbles drift lazily to the surface and disappear. "I suppose I can't write that book about the perfect crime, can I? It's so perfect that everyone would want to try it. The police would never let me publish it."

The young detective constable nodded unhappily. "And we don't want any more accidents. He's putting pressure on for more money now. He's actually poisoned some jars of baby food and put razor blades in others. It's vicious, but what can we do except pay up?"

"He put warnings into the jars, didn't he?" Whitchelo asked. "At least that's what it said on the television."

"Hah! He put a strip of metal label with a warning printed on it. Of course it sank to the bottom of the jar. The mother only found the label *after* she'd fed the baby. By then the poor child was spitting blood. Vicious!" Martin Evans repeated. "And of course now it's become public there are lots of loonies trying to copy the blackmailer. You wouldn't believe what they've been putting in food – drawing pins, glass, fuse wire . . . mind you, some phone the supermarket and lie about poisoning the food just to try to make a bit of money. They all get caught."

"Not as clever as the original then?" Whitchelo asked.

"You sound as if you admire the man," the young detective said bitterly.

The man held up a large hand. "I wouldn't say that. But you have to admit he has a good brain."

"He's got a twisted brain, Rod. And I only wish we could have caught him."

Chief Superintendent Fleming loosened his tie. The room was pretty full and getting hotter. He called out, "Can I have your attention, please?"

The men and women turned towards him and looked at him curiously. "Some of you may know that I am Chief Superintendent Fleming of Scotland Yard. I'm in charge of the baby-food blackmail case. You probably also know that the police haven't had a great deal of success in nailing the villain."

There was a mumble of agreement from Fleming's audience. "That's why we're bringing you lot in from Special Branch. It's not simply that the ordinary Regional Crime Squads have failed. It's that we suspect he's getting information directly from police sources. In Special Branch you don't usually mix with regional squad officers. The operation you are involved with will be codenamed 'Agincourt' and it's *top secret*."

The chief superintendent gave a detailed description of the case so far. "Any questions?" he finished.

A woman in the second row raised a hand. "I'm DC Susan Digby, sir. How are you planning to catch him this time? I mean, in Special Branch we don't have three thousand officers, do we?"

"No, Susan, but our villainous friend is getting careless now. It seems word has got back to him that we're giving up on the chase. That's exactly what I wanted him to think. He believes he doesn't need to travel the country to make money. He's sticking to London now. We'll watch the main London cash machines on the 20th and 21st of October and hopefully get him that way."

"But what are we looking for?" Susan Digby persisted.

Fleming looked around the room at fifty pairs of

knowing eyes. "Anything suspicious. You're all experienced officers. Police routine hasn't worked so far, so now we'll try a bit of Special Branch intelligence. I don't know *exactly* what you're looking for, but I trust you'll know it when you see it." He stacked his sheets of notes neatly and slipped them into a folder marked 'Agincourt'. "If there are no more questions then I'll leave your chief superintendent to organize the details . . . and the best of luck!"

Luck was with Fleming's team that night. A careless workman cut through a computer cable operating the cash point at Uxbridge, just outside London – a machine that was *not* being watched by Special Branch. That was the machine the blackmailer chose that night.

The man stared at the small green and black screen. "Sorry, this machine is out of service. The nearest cash point is in Enfield. We apologize for any inconvenience."

The man sighed and walked back to his car.

As he pulled up outside the Enfield office his luck finally ran out. Susan Digby and a Special Branch colleague were sitting in a car across the road. They watched as the man stepped out of the car.

Susan felt a cold slug of excitement creeping up her back. "That's him," she said. "Wait till he's taken the money, then we'll arrest him."

The officers slipped quietly out of their car and waited in the shadow of a shop doorway until the man turned back to his car. As he reached for the door handle Susan stepped forward briskly and laid a hand on his arm. "Excuse me, sir, we are police officers," and she flipped open her ID.

"What do you want?" the man said. "I've done nothing wrong."

"We were wondering why you're wearing a crash helmet when you're driving a car," she said.

"In case I get wet," the man said and tried to laugh, but the sound died in his throat.

"I am arresting you on suspicion of blackmail," she said. "Would you mind telling me your name, sir?"

The man tugged the helmet off and rested it tiredly on the roof of the car. "Whitchelo. Rodney Whitchelo."

"Occupation?"

"Retired. Retired policeman," he said.

Martin Evans supped his beer miserable and alone in the pub. The barman wiped the table and said, "Your friend Rod not coming in tonight?"

"No," the young policeman said. "Not tonight . . . and not for a very long time, I'd say."

"Problems?"

"He thought he'd discovered the perfect crime," Martin said.

"But he hadn't?"

"There's no such thing."

FACT FILE

Changing sides – FACT FILE

1. Whitchelo pleaded 'Not guilty' to the charges but the jury found him guilty and the judge sentenced him to seventeen years in prison. Officers searching his flat found the typewriter on which the blackmail note had been written and some of the poison that had been placed in jars. One of Whitchelo's tricks was to phone friends and say he was at home so that he had an 'alibi' for the times when cash was being collected hundreds of miles away. Police found his mobile phone. The calls from it were traced and they matched the places where the money had been collected. They also found tapes of Whitchelo's attempts to write his book on the perfect crime. One piece of advice was "Don't get greedy". He'd already made almost £20,000 from his scheme when he was caught. If he'd stopped then he might never have been detected. It was his greed for more and more that finally led to his downfall.

2. Food manufacturers now make their jars safe by sealing them with clear plastic. No one can poison a glass jar without breaking the seal and giving the secret away.

Whitchelo's "perfect crime" is no longer possible.

3. It's not only policemen who are tempted to break the laws they are supposed to enforce. Sir Jonah Barrington was an Irish judge. When he needed money he stole it from his court. Sir Jonah got away with it for twenty years before he was eventually caught in 1830 and sent for trial in his own court.

4. Fifty years later in the USA, Roy Bean was a gambler, saloon-keeper and smuggler before he found the best job of all – as a judge! Trials were often held up while "Judge" Bean drank whisky or played cards with his friends. He made up laws to suit himself, found people guilty and fined them, then put the fines straight into his own pocket!

5. Henry Morgan was much more successful. He was a pirate who raided Spanish colonies in South America. In 1672 he was called to England to explain his crimes. He explained himself so well that he was knighted and became Sir Henry. Then he was sent back to the West Indies as the Governor of Jamaica. He had the job of detecting and punishing pirates in the region. That was quite easy for Morgan – they were his old friends. He arrested them and had them executed.

THE JEWEL THIEVES

When the police have a suspect they use "interrogation" – questioning – to try to find the truth. Professional criminals are often skilled in lying and interrogation can fail. The police have to stick to the interrogation rules: they can't beat or torture a suspect, they can't invent evidence or tell lies. But sometimes they try one or two tricks of their own to get the proof they need, especially if they belong to the Canadian police and have the reputation for "always getting their man . . ."

Toronto, Canada, 1956

"I know they're guilty," Detective Inspector Jim Collins sighed. "We *all* know they're guilty. Proving it's another thing."

"Tell me what you've got and I'll see if I can help," his superintendent said. "You're holding two men on suspicion of the jewellery store thefts, is that right?"

"Right. We've been chasing them for five weeks," Jim Collins said and sat forward in the chair. "It seemed they were really very professional. The two men walked into the jewellers' shops and asked to see the best necklaces. The assistants took them out of the display cases and started talking about them. Of course they were so keen to sell the jewels they didn't pay enough attention to what else was going on in the shop."

"The woman?"

"That's right. A blonde woman came into the shop with them, and while the men were talking she pretended to be looking around. In fact she was stealing something pretty valuable from the cases or the window display. Why, in one shop she even disconnected an alarm before she opened a case! Of course the shops didn't discover the thefts for quite some time, sometimes not till the next day," the detective said, punching the palm of his hand in irritation.

"And you had nothing to go on?" the superintendent asked.

"Descriptions. We knew one man was very thin and the other was stocky with his hair combed forward to cover his bald spot. We nicknamed them Laurel and Hardy."

The superintendent chuckled. "You showed the shop assistants photos of some of the Toronto jewel thieves?"

"Oh, yes. But Laurel and Hardy and their girlfriend are from out of town. It seemed we'd never catch them until we had a bit of good luck. A thin man and a blonde woman were arrested for suspected shoplifting in a town-centre store. We couldn't make the charge stick and we had to let them go, but . . . I'm not sure if I should be telling you this, sir," Collins said, tugging awkwardly at his shirt cuff.

"I can always pretend I didn't hear it," his senior officer said.

"One of the arresting officers found a photograph of the man and woman in a pocket when they were searched. He accidentally forgot to return it to Mr Laurel when the couple were released."

"An easy mistake to make," the superintendent said with an innocent face. "You showed the photograph to the jewellery shop assistants?"

"And they confirmed that they were the suspects. Of course we now knew who the thieves were but we had absolutely no proof. No one saw them steal the jewels, no jewels were found in their possession, and no fingerprints were left on the jewellery cases," Collins said.

"But we were able to keep a lookout for them?"

"We were. The jewellers weren't so careful. Two more thefts were reported last Friday. That's when a patrol-car driver spotted Laurel and Hardy in a grey Ford driving down the High Street. He pulled them in. They denied any knowledge about jewels and they certainly had nothing on them."

"You searched their apartment?" the senior officer asked.

"They refused to tell us where they lived. But we had two clues: a collection of three keys in Laurel's pocket and a scrap of paper that said "Hotel Room 400" with an almost invisible phone number. While Forensic worked on tracing the hotel from the phone number we looked at the car. There was a parking ticket inside dated two nights before. We went down to the street where the ticket was issued."

"What were you looking for?" the superintendent asked. "A needle in a haystack?"

Inspector Collins couldn't help but looked pleased with himself. "A door that fitted Laurel's key," he said.

"Bit of a long shot, surely?"

"But it worked. We found a block of rented rooms that it fitted. The caretaker recognized the photograph of Laurel and we found a gun in the man's room – an illegal gun. At last we had a reason to keep him in prison while we look into the jewel thefts."

"But no jewels?"

"No jewels. I said these guys were professionals. They wouldn't leave them where we could find them. Then we traced the hotel where Hardy was staying, and what did we find there?"

"Nothing?"

"Nothing. No jewels and no blonde. She must have them with her. We wheeled Hardy in and held two identity parades. The jewellers picked out Laurel and Hardy every time."

The superintendent walked across the room and poured out two cups of coffee from a percolator on the table. As he handed one to Jim Collins he said, "I see your problem. It would never stand up in court. All you can prove is that Laurel and Hardy were in the shops. There's nothing to prove that they stole anything. A good lawyer would have the case thrown out of court. No, Jim, you need the jewels."

"We've questioned them for twelve hours now. They're saying nothing. We'll have to let them go tomorrow morning. All that work and they're laughing at us."

"You questioned them separately?" the superintendent said as he sipped at the scalding black coffee.

"Of course. We haven't let them talk to each other since they were arrested. We don't want to give them the chance to compare stories. We keep hoping they'll slip up, make a mistake. But . . ."

"But they're professionals," the superintendent finished. He looked over the rim of his cup and remarked, "Perhaps it's time we stopped being so professional ourselves."

"I don't understand, sir," Jim Collins said.

"Perhaps we should get careless. Let them have a couple of cells next door to each other. When they see how careless we can be, then maybe *they'll* get a little careless. Maybe they'll talk."

Jim Collins looked into the dark steaming liquid and

tried to picture it. "There are two cells below the interview rooms. There's a third cell across the passage from them. Somebody in that third cell could hear everything they say."

"So, try it," the superintendent said.

The detective rose slowly to his feet and drained his coffee. "It hardly seems fair, sir."

"There's no law against listening to two villains having a chat, but there is a very definite law against stealing thousands of pounds' worth of jewellery. You joined the police force to stop them . . . by hook or by crook. So do it."

The man they called Laurel looked nothing like the old film comedian. This man was taller and his eyes were harder. His mouth was unsmiling, yet something about his face showed satisfaction. "They won't hold us," he said.

The man in the next cell had small, shifting eyes buried in a fat face. "What about the gun charge?"

"We'll be given bail. We'll have a hearing tomorrow morning and it's a minor offence. They don't know about our past record in Ontario. They'll ask for a couple of hundred dollars and let us go."

"And do you want us to jump bail?" the fat one asked.

"Better lose a couple of hundred dollars than let them find the jewels and lock us away for ten years!"

"So you reckon they won't find the jewels? Where are they anyway?"

The hoarse voice of the fat man echoed down the concrete row of cells. In one cell across the corridor a policeman with a notebook held his breath and waited for the answer.

"In the next block. Separated by a steel wall," the thin one replied.

Perhaps it was the soft rustle of the policeman's notebook that unsettled the man. "I wonder why they put us together in these cells. You don't suppose they're bugged, do you?"

The fat man rolled his little eyes nervously round the cell, looking for a microphone. "Nah!" he said. "They'd never think of anything as smart as that."

Detective Inspector Collins yawned. It had been a long night but he had to find those jewels before morning. The court would free the crooks and they'd vanish. The shops would lose a fortune in jewellery . . . and the Canadian police would have a black mark against them in the minds of the shopkeepers.

He stepped into the hotel to meet the manager. The man was wearing a dressing gown and his hair had a slept-in look. "Sorry to trouble you at this time of night," Collins said.

"It's morning. Three a.m. to be exact," the manager said sourly.

"Yes. You were kind enough to let us search the suspect's room this afternoon," the detective said.

"No problem. But you found nothing, did you?"

"We didn't. But we have reason to believe that the jewels may be hidden behind a steel wall. Would you know where that is?"

The manager rubbed a hand over his unshaven chin. "The whole block is divided into two by a steel wall," he explained. "Fire regulations. There's a steel wall at the end of each corridor."

"At the end of the suspect's corridor?"

"Of course."

"So, what's on the other side of the steel wall?"

The manager looked impatient. "The other half of the corridor, of course. And another block of rooms."

"So how could he hide something there?" Jim Collins asked.

"He couldn't. Unless he'd booked another room," the manager suggested.

"Did he?"

"No. The man booked Room 400, the one you searched."

"Did the man or the woman go into the other half of the building for any reason?" the detective asked desperately.

Now the manager said something which stopped the inspector's heart for half a beat. He said, "What woman?"

Jim Collins was wide awake now. "The suspect booked room 400. He had a blonde woman with him."

"No, he didn't," the manager said.

The detective slid a hand inside his jacket pocket and was pleased he'd remembered to bring the photograph with him. "So you've never seen this woman?"

"Sure I've seen that woman," the manager said.

"You told me she wasn't with the man in Room 400!" Jim Collins cried.

"She wasn't. She came in yesterday and took a room in the other half of the building. Room 207, I think."

The detective cursed himself. "Why didn't you tell me the suspect was alone?"

"You never asked!" the angry manager replied.

"Sorry! Sorry!" Jim Collins said. "Could we go to Room 207 now?"

"She'll be asleep," the manager objected.

"Shame," the detective snapped.

After the blonde woman had been wakened and hurried off to the police station for questioning, the team of detectives got to work. "These crooks are professionals," Jim Collins told his men.

"So are we, sir," one of his men assured him. "If a piece of gold has rested in this room we'll find its shadow."

Jim Collins sank tiredly against the door post and let them carry out the search. The curtains were pulled open and the pearl-grey light of early morning spilled into the room. There wasn't much time left.

But when the searchers reached the couch under the window they struck gold . . . and diamond and platinum. Ten rings and a $5,000 watch were enough for the inspector to start with.

He drove through the empty streets too quickly and arrived as the manager of Howard's Credit Jewellers was having breakfast. "Can you identify any of these as your property?" he asked.

The manager could. Collins gave him just ten minutes to shave and dress. The man was still chewing toast as they raced towards the courtroom.

The unsmiling man that the detectives called Laurel sat in the dock of the courtroom. That faint expression of confidence was on his face. It was still there when Inspector Jim Collins stepped into the witness box and faced the court's questions.

"And have you recovered any of the jewellery, Inspector?" the judge asked.

Jim Collins looked at the crooks and it was his turn to smile. "Yes, your honour. We have a stolen watch and ten rings."

The judge looked at the defendants. "I believe you have a case to answer. You will go on trial for the theft of jewellery. No bail."

As Detective Inspector Collins wandered out of the courtroom he was greeted by his superintendent. "Coffee?"

"I'd rather have a few hours' sleep," he groaned.

"So our plan worked?"

"Yes, sir."

"Who was it said 'Cheats never beats'?"

"I don't know, sir . . . but they were wrong."

Criminal records – FACT FILE

1. The thieves known to Collins as 'Laurel and Hardy' were sentenced to six years in jail each. Two years later a jewellery shop assistant reported a theft and described a suspicious character who had been hanging around that day. It happened that Collins was asked to deal with the case. "Sounds just like a guy we jailed two years ago," he said. "But he's in jail." He checked anyway. 'Laurel' had been released early for good conduct . . . and gone straight back to the shoplifting racket. His bad luck in being matched against Collins again meant he went back to prison for the remaining four years.

2. Normally the police would hope to trace someone who repeats a crime from their records. Every time an arrest is made the criminal has his or her fingerprints and photograph taken. Some police forces then add details of the people they commit crimes with (their 'associates') and the skills the criminal has.

3. Police may also keep examples of a

criminal's handwriting. In a 1956 American kidnap case the criminal was trapped with the help of police records. Police passed on his ransom note to handwriting experts. They checked all written confessions in the files, reading more than a million samples over six weeks, but in the end they found the one that matched.

4. Modern science can identify individuals from their voice. A criminal's 'voice-print' can be taken, printed and stored like a fingerprint. Even if a person tried to disguise their voice, the voice-print can recognize it. This is very useful for police checking telephone calls which are threatening or which are made by a kidnapper demanding a ransom. There is an interesting case of voice-testing in the Bible, thousands of years before electronic voice-prints. The leader Jephthah wanted to detect the enemy Ephraimites in his group of followers. He asked everyone to say the word 'Shibboleth'. The Ephraimites pronounced it 'Sibboleth' (without the 'h'). Jephthah's detective work was a success!

5. Samples of a criminal's blood can now be taken and matched to any tiny scrap of hair, blood or skin left at the scene of a crime. This is know as 'DNA printing' and is said by some scientists to be as reliable as a finger-

print, though twins will have the same DNA print. Unfortunately mistakes can be made by testers. At least one man had his life ruined with a prison sentence where the only evidence against him was a faulty DNA test. Yet in 1994 the law in Britain was changed to allow police to keep DNA test records of criminals.

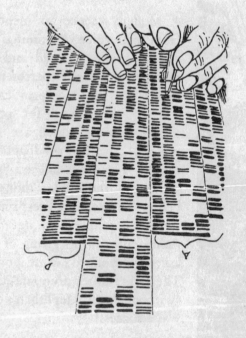

THE GHOSTLY DETECTIVE

Sometimes the best detective in the world can fail to solve a crime, then the solution comes in a strange and unexpected way. It is almost as if the victim of the crime has returned from the grave to provide the final clue.

Kent, England, 1922

"I've a strange story to tell," the old man said. He was shrunken and grey inside a worn black suit but there was a fierce intelligence in the sad, shadowed eyes.

Superintendent Edward Carlin was too busy to listen to strange stories. "I know you're busy," the old man said, as if he could read the policeman's mind, "but I will try to keep my story brief."

The superintendent relaxed and invited the man to take the battered armchair while he sat down again behind an office desk littered with papers, files and forms.

"My name is George Tombe," the old man began, "and I am the vicar of a small church in Sydenham. I live there with my wife, Victoria, and we have a son, Eric. At least," he said, looking away from the policeman to hide some sudden pain, "we *had* a son called Eric. Victoria and I have every reason to believe we will never see him again."

"Perhaps the 'Missing Persons' register at your regional police headquarters would be able to help you, Reverend Tombe," the policeman said.

"Ah, no. We have no hope of finding Eric alive, you understand. We believe he is dead. It is simply our wish that we may find his body and give it a Christian burial. I have come to Scotland Yard because our local police said that you have the sort of information I may need."

"We have crime records, Reverend. Are you suggesting

your son is the victim of a crime?"

"Precisely," the old man said with a curious bow of the head. "I have done all the detective work that I can possibly do, but I lack your contacts . . . and your experience, of course. I am coming to you as a last resort."

"Tell me what you have found," Superintendent Carlin said, "and I'll see if we can help."

"Thank you, Superintendent," the vicar said, opening the black leather briefcase on his knee. "This is the last letter we received from Eric," he said as he passed the note across the desk.

"Dated Tuesday the seventeenth of April last year," the policeman read. "*I shall be coming to see you on Saturday.*" He looked up. "He never arrived?"

"He never arrived. His flat in the West End of London was deserted. It seemed he had vanished without taking any clothes. We placed adverts in local and national newspapers, but there was no response. We informed the local police but they said, as no doubt *you* would say, that hundreds of people go missing every year and that most of them turn up after a couple of months."

"They sent enquiries to hospitals and searched accident records, did they?" Carlin asked.

Again the vicar bowed his head. "They did indeed. I have no complaints on that score. They did what they could. They could not, however, spare the time to search for my son. I knew I'd have to do that myself."

Superintendent Carlin had to admire the vicar as the old man told his story of the search for his son Eric. He'd arrived in London and begun by knocking on the doors of his son's neighbours. The neighbours all confirmed that

Eric had been missing since about April and one or two were able to give him the names of people his son had known.

For three months the old man trailed the streets of London, riding nervously on new motor buses or being rattled through dingy tunnels on underground trains. But each journey ended in the same way, at a dead end.

Every weekend he would return to his parish in Sydenham and report back to Victoria. Every weekend he would have to watch her disappointed face as he told of his failure to track down their son. "Perhaps you should stop now. You are wearing yourself out," she would say.

"One more try," he would insist. "One more try."

That last Monday morning he decided to talk to the barber who cut Eric's hair. Barbers are chatty people. If he remembered Eric then he might remember him talking about his plans.

"We talked about the war, sir," the barber told the old man. "And after the war I understand Mister Eric went into the motor trade. I believe he had some money in the bank, which he invested in two garages."

"Do you remember where they were?"

"No, sir. But I understand they did not succeed. From what Mister Eric said, I think his partner was as much to blame as anything. He was not a very sound businessman."

"And do you remember the name of this partner?" the vicar asked eagerly.

"Afraid not, sir . . . though he did come here once."

"He came *here*? That's a coincidence," the vicar said.

"Not at all, sir. Mister Eric recommended us to the gentleman. We put that sort of introduction in our little reference book, sir."

"And could I see this book?" the Reverend Tombe asked.

"Here we are, sir," the barber said, opening the small red book. "Ernest Dyer's the name. His address is 'The Welcomes', Kenley . . . and it says here, 'Introduced by Mr Eric Tombe.'"

Superintendent Carlin interrupted the old man's story at this point. "Dyer, you say? That name's familiar. Excuse me a moment." He picked up the telephone on his desk and dialled. "Edmonds? I think we have a file on someone called Dyer, don't we? Ernest Dyer. Can you bring it to my office?" He replaced the phone on its cradle and said, "Sorry, Reverend. Carry on."

The vicar had visited 'The Welcomes' the next day. The bleak and blackened skeleton of a farmhouse stood in a shabby yard. The whole place had a gloomy and neglected air about it. A woman came from the stable block to meet him. "I'm looking for an Ernest Dyer," he said, raising his hat.

"Aren't we all!" the woman said sourly. "I'm his wife. He disappeared some time last month. He owes a lot of people a lot of money. I suppose you're after some yourself, are you?"

"No, no. I am trying to trace my son, Eric Tombe," the old man explained.

The woman softened a little. "Ah, you're Eric's father, are you? Come into the stables and I'll try to help you."

"The stables?"

"That's where we live now, since the house burned down."

"How unfortunate."

"Hah! Unfortunate!" she snorted as she led the way

105

towards the block of stone buildings. "Another one of Ernest's little plans that went wrong. We bought that house for £5,000 and Ernest insured it for £12,000. When it burned down the insurance company refused to pay."

"Why was that?"

"The insurance inspector spotted one or two petrol cans lying around and accused Ernest of burning his own house down. Ernest didn't argue."

"Oh, dear!" the vicar said, worrying about the man his son had been mixed up with.

"Look, I have to be honest, Mr Tombe; I haven't seen your Eric since Easter. You knew he had a big row with Ernest, did you?"

"No, I didn't."

"Eric accused Ernest of forging his signature on some of their business cheques. Knowing Ernest, that was probably true. Ernest and Eric went away after that. They split the partnership and I haven't seen them since. Maybe the bank will have some record of your son, Mr Tombe," she suggested.

"Do you have their address?" he asked.

Mrs Dyer found a letter from the manager and the Reverend Tombe copied it down. "And you have no idea where Eric went?" he asked.

"Ernest showed me a telegram from Eric. It said 'Have been called overseas.' Does that help?"

The vicar frowned. "No. I'm sorry, Mrs Dyer, but Eric never used the word 'overseas' in his life. I don't want to call your husband a liar . . ."

"Why not? Everyone else does."

"I just can't believe that Eric sent that telegram."

"Can't say I blame you," the woman agreed.

There didn't seem much else she could tell him. The old man crossed the icy mud of the farmyard and set off down the track to the village. He reached the bank before it closed that day.

The bank manager was dressed in a smart black tail coat and was smooth as the bank's marble floor. "No need to worry, Mr Tombe. We had a letter from your son just a month or so ago."

"May I see it?"

"It is not normal practice . . . but I suppose there is no harm, if it will set your mind at rest," the manager smiled. He slid the letter across to the vicar.

The Reverend Tombe looked up. "I'm sorry," he said, "very sorry. But this letter is not from my son. It is not his handwriting or his signature."

"But it asks for all his money to be transferred to Mr Ernest Dyer," the manager gasped. "Mr Dyer has since emptied the account. If this letter is a forgery, then Dyer has robbed your son!"

The old man said simply, "I fear he may have done more than simply robbed him."

Superintendent Carlin studied the file for a few minutes, then said, "It's not good news, Reverend. The Yorkshire police had a report of a man who was attempting a business fraud in Scarborough. Detective Inspector Abbot went to investigate and met the man in a hotel. The man offered to go to his room to settle the matter, but on the way upstairs he reached inside his jacket pocket. Abbot thought he was trying to destroy some evidence. He grabbed the man and they struggled. In the struggle Abbot discovered that the suspect was in fact reaching for a gun.

The gun went off accidentally and the suspect died instantly."

"That man was Ernest Dyer?"

"He was. When the inspector searched the room he found a passport in the name of Eric Tombe . . . and a hundred cheques with Tombe's signature on them," the Superintendent said, studying his file. "At the time the Yorkshire police made no attempt to trace this Eric Tombe. They thought that he was just an invention of Dyer's – a secret identity if he ever needed to escape to the continent." He looked up from the reports. "This seems to confirm your worst fears, Reverend."

"Indeed," the old man sighed. "Dyer is – or was – a killer. He had argued with my son over the cheques and no doubt killed him. Then he began forging Eric's signature on bank letters and cheques in order to continue taking my son's money."

"That seems a likely course of events," the policeman agreed. "You have done a magnificent job of piecing together your son's story, Reverend, a wonderful piece of detective work. My own men couldn't have done better. It's only a pity that Dyer's death means we may never find what you want – your son's body."

Then the old man said something. He spoke so matter-of-factly that Superintendent Carlin wondered if he'd heard him correctly. "What did you say?"

"I said, we *know* where Eric's body is. We simply need your help in uncovering it."

"Then why —"

"I hadn't quite finished my story, Superintendent. I returned home from the bank with the news about Eric. My wife and I talked it over for a long time and we persuaded ourselves that he must be dead. But then Victoria began to have dreams – the strangest and most horrifying dreams. And in these dreams she saw Eric's body. It was lying at the bottom of a well. At first I thought it was just a nightmare, but night after night the dream returned. I believe it is not a dream but a message from the afterlife, Superintendent. No, I don't expect you to believe in such nonsense, but just in case there *is* something in it, could I ask you to investigate the possibility?"

Just twice in his life Superintendent Carlin was lost for words. The first time was when Reverend Tombe told his story of the dream. The second was when he drove down to The Welcomes to question Mrs Dyer about Eric Tombe's disappearance. She couldn't tell him much more than she had told the vicar.

"One final question, Mrs Dyer," the policeman said as he was folding away his notebook. "Would you have such a thing as a well on your farm?"

The woman shrugged. "A disused well, Superintendent. There are five on our land. Do you think Ernest hid something there? It wouldn't surprise me. Now you mention it, I was alone in the farm one night when I heard stones being dropped down the well behind the barn. When I went outside with the dog I saw a man in the shadows."

"Who was it, Mrs Dyer?"

"It was my husband. He told me not to come near, but he never did explain what he was doing that night."

"If you don't mind, Mrs Dyer, we'll search that well," the policeman said.

"Dust to dust and ashes to ashes," the Reverend said. "I have buried many people in my time as a vicar. I never thought I'd see the day when I'd have to bury poor Eric."

"At least you found him, sir. You and your wife and that remarkable dream," Superintendent Carlin said in the cool calm of the church after the service.

The old man dabbed at the tears that were running down his face. "No, Superintendent. He was found for us by someone far greater than Victoria or me, someone that we'll have to meet one day. As the poet William Cowper said, 'God moves in a mysterious way, His wonders to perform.'"

EPILOGUE

The stories in this book are all about unusual cases of detective work, cases where the investigator had to solve a puzzle to clear up a crime. That's what many people think of when they picture detective work, but most detectives will tell you that patience, persistence and the ability to ask the right questions are just as important as solving puzzles.

In the last two hundred years science has been helping the detective more and more. Unfortunately, criminals soon learn about science. The scientist discovers finger-printing, the detective discovers a use for it in crime-fighting, and the criminal discovers a use for gloves! The scientist invents the video camera, the detective discovers its use in keeping an electronic eye on valuables, and the criminal discovers a new use for a mask! And so it goes on.

But it's not all a losing battle for the detective. Criminals have been bringing misery to their victims for thousands of years, yet the oldest aid to detection is still one of the best – the witness. Two-thirds of solved crimes are unravelled with the help of a witness – someone like you. Police can't be everywhere all of the time, so they rely on the public informing them of unusual or suspicious happenings.

You can be the detective's best friend. In the world of true detective stories, *you* are one of the main characters.

TRUE
SPY
STORIES

Thanks to the Portgordon Cultural Heritage Group for the original story of "The Apple Spy"

CONTENTS

INTRODUCTION

My name is Bond, James Bond, but you can call me 007.

Well, that's not true. My name is *not* James Bond, and James Bond never existed. But we can all dream and spying seems a dream job … *if* you believe all you see in the cinema and read in the books.

Spies seem so glamorous. Their lives are full of excitement and they are always such heroes! They are working for their country against an evil enemy who is out to destroy them. They are snatching secrets from under the noses of some foreign secret police and bringing them home. They are our guardian angels.

Of course enemy spies are *not* so glamorous, are they? They are traitors who sneak about, lying, murdering and stealing from our country. Enemy spies will use any low and dirty trick you can imagine to get their hands on our secrets. They are the worst devils of our nightmares.

Spies are angels – when they are on our side. Spies are devils when they work for the enemy. What is the truth? Would *you* like to be a spy? There is only one way to find out. Forget about James Bond for a while. Look at some *true* spy stories. Study the people who have lived and died as spies, the way they work, the sort of things they had to do.

Spies have been around for thousands of years. Did you know that there are spy stories in the Bible? In one story a Persian called Zopyrus wanted to get inside Babylon and let his Persian army in. He walked up to the gates of Babylon and said, "I want to join you. I hate the Persians. I tried to talk them out of attacking Babylon so they cut off my ears and my nose and whipped me till I bled."

The Babylonians believed Zopyrus and let him into the city – as soon as he had the chance the sneaky Zopyrus opened the gates of Babylon and let in his Persian friends.

How could the Babylonians have been so stupid as to believe this lying spy? Because they saw he had no nose, no ears and his back was raw with whipping. If *you* saw this horrid sight then wouldn't you believe he hated the Persians for doing that to him?

The *truth* about Zopyrus the spy is too amazing to believe. Zopyrus whipped himself, cut off his own nose and lopped his own ears just to get into Babylon.

What a hero – to the Persians.

Could *you* do that for *your* country? Can you imagine James Bond cutting off his nose? No! Because James Bond stories are make-believe and Zopyrus's is a true spy story. If you want to know more true spy stories then read them here.

LEXANDER THE GREATEST

Spying is about gathering information and stealing secrets. Leaders want to know what their enemies are up to. In the 1500s, Queen Elizabeth had one of the world's first spy organizations run by her spy-master Sir Francis Walsingham. But, before that, rulers had to come up with their own plots. Alexander the Great was a master of secret schemes. Some say he murdered his own father to get control of the kingdom. He then went on to conquer Greece and Persia. He was the master of the greatest empire in the world, but he still wasn't safe. Alexander had no spy-master like Sir Francis Walsingham. He had to do it all for himself…

Date: 327 BC

Place: Persia

The man was barefoot and dirty. His hair was matted and his body was covered in sores. His body was hunched and he looked over his shoulder every few steps. At last he arrived at the magnificent silk tent. "I've come to see the emperor," he croaked.

The guard looked at him with disgust but lowered his spear and nodded for the man to enter the tent. Alexander was lying on a couch and studying a map when the shabby man slid in. He looked up sharply. The emperor was a young man but the strain of the fighting and the constant danger had given him hard lines at the edge of his large eyes and firm mouth. "Did anyone see you?"

"No, sir," the man said in a soft whine.

Alexander rested his hand on the hilt of the dagger at his belt. "It had better be important," he said menacingly.

"It is, sir."

"Quickly then, what is it?"

"It's some of your men, sir. They're not happy."

The emperor swung his feet to the floor and planted a

strong hand on the map. "I have given them Greece and its wealth," he said and jabbed at the map with his finger. He moved it to the right. "We've conquered Persia and its riches. Now we're going to take India and enough of its treasures to make them rich for life," he said, sweeping his fingers to the south-east. "What more do they want?"

"They want to go home, sir."

Alexander's lip curled in a sneer. "Over my dead body."

The man in the tattered tunic clasped his hands tightly. "I think that's what they are planning, sir," he whispered.

His master snorted. "So, it's come to that, has it? They plan to murder me and run home to their dear little wives and mothers, do they?"

"That's what I heard them plan, sir."

"Which men are leading the plot?"

"Oh, I can't tell you that, sir. They wouldn't let a camp-follower like me into their great tents, sir. I only know what I heard through the tent walls."

"Didn't you recognize the voices?"

The man shook his head sadly. "No, sir."

"Get out," Alexander ordered. As the man backed slowly towards the door the emperor reached into a leather pouch and took out a coin. He threw it on to the floor. The man snatched it with a stained hand and ran out into the night. Alexander lay back on his couch, closed his eyes and rested a hand on his brow. The only sound was the sputtering of oil lamps and the distant barking of dogs on guard at the edge of the camp.

After a long while he rose slowly and walked to the door of the tent. "Fetch General Parmenion," he snapped. The guard woke from his doze and pulled himself to attention.

Parmenion had been asleep when his leader's message

came. He threw on a tunic and sandals and limped through the rows of tents by the light of the dying camp-fires. He combed his grey hair with his fingers and entered Alexander's tent. He saluted quickly and waited.

"Parmenion," Alexander said warmly. "Sit down, my friend."

The general sat on the couch, while Alexander paced the floor of the tent. "Sorry to wake you."

"I'm used to it," the old soldier laughed. "You've had one of your ideas, I suppose."

"Yes, Parmenion. I am worried about the men being so far from home. We've been away from Greece for two years now. Some of the men must be getting a little homesick."

"They worry about their families, of course," Parmenion said.

"Don't we all?"

"I have my son Nicias alongside me," the general smiled. "I'm one of the lucky ones."

"You *are*. But I thought it might be good for the men to get in touch with their families. I thought I'd arrange to have a wagon sent home to deliver their letters."

Parmenion shrugged. "We've tried it before, but the wagons have always been attacked and robbed by bandits on land or pirates at sea. Writing those letters was just a waste of time."

"But this time it would be different. This time I would send it with a strong armed guard."

Parmenion gave a broad smile. "That is marvellous, sir. It will be very popular with the men."

Alexander looked up sharply. "Am I not popular now?"

Parmenion's smile faded. "Oh! Of course, Emperor! The men love you!"

"*All* of the men?"

"*All* of them," Parmenion cried.

Alexander slapped a hand on his general's shoulder. "You are a good man, Parmenion. Too good at times. You see only the good in our friends. You don't see the bad. But I trust you, Parmenion. Of all the officers in this army you're the only one I trust."

"Thank you, sir."

"I'll announce the mail wagon tomorrow at the planning meeting. It will leave tomorrow evening."

The next morning, Alexander explained his plan to send letters back to Greece and told his officers that the day would be a rest day. They could spend the time writing. "I promise you, the letters will be safe in my care. I have selected the men who will escort the wagon. There are no better men in this army."

As evening fell on the dusty plain the mail wagon was loaded and was placed in the middle of a convoy of heavily armed soldiers with their own baggage and supplies wagons. The order was given to leave and the company set off slowly towards the setting sun.

After half an hour, the camp was out of sight and the road took the wagons into some low hills. A man sat on top of one hill and watched them pass below him, then he rode slowly down towards the lumbering horses. The driver stopped and saluted. "Good evening, Emperor."

"Good evening, Captain," Alexander said, and he smiled grimly. "Stop here for a while. Give the men food but no wine – I want them awake for the rest of the night. And light some torches so I can read."

The company dismounted and began to gather wood for fires, while their emperor pulled the parcels of letters from the wagon and began to open them. After an hour Alexander had two piles of letters. He picked up the smaller pile and called the commander of the company across to him. "These letters here are the ones that have the information I want. The writers have told their loved ones all about a plot to kill me and return home. Some have very kindly listed all the men who are part of the plot. Of course they will have to die."

"Yes, sir."

"I've made a list of the names. I want you to leave the wagons here and return to the camp on horseback with me. We'll take these men while they are asleep. There will be no need for any trials. You will bring them to me one at a time, I will listen to their confessions in my tent, and then you will take them outside and execute them. Do you understand?"

"Perfectly, Emperor."

"Then let's make ready."

It was deep into the night when the sleepy and confused plotters were dragged from their beds and held under close guard until Alexander was ready to see them. Parmenion hurried from the comfort of his bed for the second night running and dashed into Alexander's tent. "What is happening, Emperor?"

Alexander held up one of the letters. "We have traitors in our midst, Parmenion."

The general read the letter quickly and his face creased with pain. "Hippothales? A traitor? Who'd have thought it?" he cried.

"I told you that you trusted people too much, Parmenion. But it is there in his own writing. I have to execute him and the other men on my list."

"Of course you do," the general said. "They deserve it."

"I'm glad you agree," Alexander said softly. Then he called, "Bring in the first traitor!"

The guards led a young officer into the tent. His face was bruised and bleeding from the struggle he'd put up when he was arrested. Parmenion looked at the young man and turned pale. "Nicias!" he moaned.

"Yes," Alexander nodded. "Your son." The emperor looked at the prisoner. "Have you anything to say, Nicias?"

The young man raised his chin so he looked down on the emperor. "You are a tyrant and an evil man, Alexander. You are not satisfied with conquering half of the world. You want it all!"

Alexander nodded slowly. "I conquered half the world by being ruthless with anyone who stood in my way. And that's how I'll conquer the other half. You'll have to die so I can live."

"I'm not afraid."

Alexander laughed suddenly. "Hah! And *I'm* not afraid to die *some* day. I'm just not ready to die *yet*. It's such a waste."

"Then let him live," Parmenion put in quickly.

The emperor frowned. "Moments ago you agreed that these traitors should all die."

Parmenion hung his head. When he raised it again his eyes were filled with tears. His son was being hauled out of the tent and he took a step to follow. Two of Alexander's bodyguards seized his arms and held him back. Alexander walked across to him and stood very close. "If I have the son killed, then the father will have a duty to avenge his son … won't you, Parmenion?"

"Yes."

"So, even though you didn't plot against me, I will have to have you killed too. You understand, don't you?"

"Yes."

The emperor's large, dark eyes softened. "Nicias was wrong, my friend. It's not *enough* to be ruthless and cruel. If you want to rule the world you need something else. You need cunning. You must trust no one, Parmenion. Especially not the ones who *say* they are your friends. Watch their every move and set traps. Spy out their secrets and know everything. That's the way to rule the world, Parmenion." He stretched out his arms and held the old general close for a few moments. "Goodbye, my friend. Goodbye."

Alexander was so upset by the execution of Parmenion and the other plotters that he refused to eat for a week. In the end he was force-fed by his friends.

The emperor wasn't the only famous person to become a spy. There have been many people who were famous for other things but were also spies. People like London Lord Mayor Dick Whittington, who spied for his king on foreign travels and England's first great poet, Geoffrey Chaucer, who wrote spy reports in a secret code. These are just a few of the ones we know about…

1. Mithradates the Great, 132–63 BC. This teenage king of Turkey fled from assassins and disguised himself as a beggar. He had learned 22 languages by the age of 14 – always useful for a spy – and wandered through Turkish cities studying their defences. After a few years he knew all about those defences and the weaknesses of the cities. He returned and, with his small army, easily overran the cities and reclaimed his throne. Mithradates's mother and brother had been ruling the country – he had them executed.

2. Marcus Licinius Crassus, 115–53 BC. This Roman ruled the Empire alongside Julius Caesar. He set up schools for slaves and the educated slaves were given jobs with the most important Romans. They also spied on those top Romans and reported their secrets to Crassus. He used those secrets to make himself rich and to keep himself safe from his enemies. When Crassus led an army against Parthia he didn't bother to use spies and was defeated. His head was cut off and his mouth filled with molten gold.

F A C T F I L E

3. King Alfred the Great, AD 849–899. Alfred was the leader of the Saxons in England at a time when the Danes were taking over the country. One story says that Alfred dressed himself as a minstrel and wandered into the Danish camp. He entertained them and stayed for their feast where they talked about their battle plans. Next day Alfred slipped out of the camp and prepared the Saxon army to defeat the plans he'd overheard. Sadly, this story was first written down 500 years after Alfred's death so there's no way of checking if it's true.

4. Christopher Marlowe, 1564–1593. This playwright could have been as great as William Shakespeare. The trouble is he seemed to enjoy spying as much as writing. He worked for Elizabeth I's spy-master, Sir Francis Walsingham, and his job was to uncover Catholic plots against the Queen. Like many other spies his masters suspected he was working secretly for the enemy – the Catholics. In a meeting with three of Walsingham's spies, Marlowe was stabbed in the eye and died. The spies claimed it was a quarrel – some historians think Marlowe was executed because his spy-masters mistrusted him.

5. Daniel Defoe, 1660–1731. This English writer was not popular with the government because he wrote offensive things about them. After a spell in prison he offered to work for the government and train spies. These spies would report on exactly who was making trouble in Britain. Defoe's secret agents were trained to mix with the population and seem quite ordinary – then betray their friends. It was Britain's first real secret service. He was able to give up spying when one of his books became a great success – the famous *Robinson Crusoe*.

6. Benjamin Franklin, 1706–90. A famous scientist who tried to be a double agent. He was one of the founders of the American spy network and pretended to be working for them in the War of Independence. In fact, he was passing on their secrets to the British. Then, when it was clear that the Americans were going to win the war, he rejoined the American side. One of the American leaders, John Quincy Adams, suspected Franklin of betraying his country but he didn't have enough evidence.

Franklin survived to become a hero of American science.

7. Sir Robert Baden-Powell, 1857–1941. From 1880 till 1902 this army officer used his skill as an actor to enter enemy territory in disguise. In Hercegovina he pretended to be a butterfly collector while collecting plans of enemy gun positions, and in Hamburg he pretended to be a drunk to get details of German warships. He became a spy-trainer, using Zulus to spy on the Dutch during the Boer Wars in South Africa. He wrote a book called *Aids to Scouting* in 1899 and it was used to train boy-soldiers. This later gave him the idea of creating the Boy Scout organization and that's what he is remembered for.

8. Mata Hari, 1876–1917. This Dutch woman was a very popular dancer in the early 1900s and had many important admirers. Mata Hari was able to learn French and British secrets and was accused of selling them to Germany during World War I. Mata Hari offered to work for the French Secret Service but they accused her of betraying them. The French put her on trial and she was sentenced to death by firing squad. Bravely she refused to have a blindfold. The truth is that she never learned any dangerous secrets and never betrayed anyone.

THE CULPER RING

Think of spies and you think of agents living with the enemy, secret messages written in code with invisible ink and clever ways of arranging for letters to be picked up. Not many true spy stories have these interesting features ... but one story has them all! The place was New York in 1780. The victims were the British Army. The spies were the Americans who wanted independence from British rule. This is the story of one vital message that got through, thanks to a group of American spies who became known as the Culper Ring.

The woman was small and slim. Her bright eyes sparkled with excitement as she ran up the stairs to the room above the store and threw open the door. "Robert! Robert!" she cried. "I've heard the most amazing thing."

Robert Townsend looked up from the table. His red-brown hair was cut short and pulled back into a ribbon at the back of his head. He raised his cleft chin and looked down his long nose at her. Without speaking, he rose to his feet, crossed to the door and looked down the stairs. Then he closed the door quietly and returned to his seat at the table. His tired eyes had dark shadows under them and made him look older than his 25 years.

"Now, quietly, my dear. What have you heard?"

She sat across the table from him and leaned forward eagerly. "The British are planning to attack our friends the French at Newport! We have to warn the French!"

Robert looked at her calmly. "They will want to strike before the French can join up with our American forces," he nodded. "It would be disastrous for us. Are you sure of this?"

"The British major told me himself. He was boasting about it!"

"Then we must send a message to our general to warn him," Robert said calmly. He walked to a cupboard and took out a small ink bottle, a quill pen and a blank sheet of paper. The woman watched as he dipped the quill in the pot and began to write. She watched, fascinated, as his pen touched the paper and the liquid vanished. "What are you saying?" she demanded.

He spoke as he wrote. "To 321. This 356 is to say that 355 reports our friends in 727 plan an advance on 644. Take 356 to 711 without delay."

She smiled and nodded. "To the spy chief. This letter is to say that 355 – that's me – reports our friends in New York – that's the British – plan an advance on the French. Take letter to our general without delay."

When he had finished the sheet of paper looked as blank as before he had started. "You've done well," he said, but still he didn't smile at the bright-eyed woman. "Stay here. 724 is due here in an hour."

Robert walked slowly down the stairs into the store and took his place behind the counter. When his assistant, Henry Oakman, left to have some dinner, Robert took the sheet of paper from under his jacket and placed it on the counter. He took a packet of paper from a shelf, opened it carefully and counted out 19 sheets. Robert placed his own sheet at number 20 and slipped it back into the packet, then sealed it.

Oakman had returned and was serving some British soldiers when Austin Roe strolled into the shop. He grinned at the soldiers. "Morning, gentlemen!" he said cheerfully and raised his hat to them. Then he turned to Robert Townsend and brought out a slip of paper. He slid it across the counter, under the noses of the British soldiers and said, "My order, Master Townsend."

Robert picked up the paper and tried to control the trembling in his hand. All that appeared on the paper were the words, "Will you please send one ream of letter paper, the same as the last shipment." The storekeeper knew that between the lines of the message was another written in invisible ink. He folded the note carelessly and stuffed it into a pouch at the front of his apron. Then he reached beneath the counter and found the packet of paper he'd prepared earlier. He passed it across to Austin Roe.

"There you are, Master Roe," he said. He couldn't say too much with the British in the shop. "I guess it will be an urgent order, is it? You'll be hurrying back with it, won't you?"

He pulled a face. "I have just ridden 50 miles for this order and now you want me to ride straight back?"

Robert's face was wooden. "That's right. You'll want to be in Setauket before nightfall. There are all sorts of strange folk out on the roads these days."

"Bandits, you mean?" Austin cried. The British soldiers looked at him and he smiled back. "I know I'm safe so long as the British army is in control."

The soldiers nodded seriously. Austin Roe turned away from them so they didn't see the huge wink he gave to Robert Townsend. "Give my regards to your lovely wife," he said happily and walked out of the shop with the packet of paper underneath his arm.

He walked along the waterfront towards the tavern. Robert's shop was in a good position there. He could stand behind his counter and watch all the British ships that arrived and left. That was what usually went in his reports. Austin Roe guessed that today there was something more urgent. He collected a fresh horse from the tavern and had a hasty meal before he rode quickly out of the city on the road to Setauket.

The sentry on the road from New York stopped Austin, as he knew he would. "Where are you going?"

"Good afternoon, Sergeant! A fine day, isn't it?"

The British soldier was not going to be fooled by Austin Roe's cheerful greeting. "I asked you where you were going."

"Back home to Setauket. I've just been collecting supplies from New York. Paper for my master's business. You can examine it if you like."

"Make sure you go straight home," the sour-faced soldier said, and let him through.

Austin's excitement gave him all the energy he needed to climb off his horse four hours later and run up the steps of the front porch to his house. "Good journey?" his wife called.

"Safe enough. But the British are nervous about something. They're checking everyone." He laid the packet of paper on his table, looked up at her worried face and smiled. He patted the parcel. "It's safe enough," he said and began to open it. He pulled out the 20th sheet. It looked as blank as the rest but he sniffed at it and the faint scent of chemicals told him it was the right one. He folded it carefully and placed it inside his jacket. "I'll pass it on and be back for supper in 20 minutes," he said.

"It'll be ready," his wife told him.

Austin walked to the end of his row of houses and opened the gate into a field of cows. He'd been away for a day in New York – no one would be surprised to see him checking his beasts in the field he rented from little Abraham Woodhull.

Austin checked each animal patiently then made his way across to the far corner of the field. There was a hollow there and he was out of sight of prying eyes. He dropped quickly to his knees, brushed earth away with his hand and uncovered the lid of a wooden box. He flipped up the lid, dropped the paper inside, closed it and covered it with soil again. Then he returned home to his hard-earned supper.

No one would be surprised to see Abraham Woodhull cross the field half an hour later. But everyone who knew him would be amazed to know he was American Agent 722, code-named Culper, and head of the Culper spy ring. Abraham was a pale-faced, trembling little man who was scared of his own shadow. He lived in terror of being discovered and that terror often drove him to his sickbed. That evening his whole body shook as he crossed the field, slipped the paper from its hiding-place and hurried back to his room in the lodging house. He passed the door to the room where two British officers lived and his trembling legs almost failed to carry him on up the stairs to his own room.

It was cool now that the sun had set, but Abraham was sweating as he locked the door and turned up the wick on his oil lamp. He took a bottle of liquid from his desk and carefully brushed it over the blank paper. Slowly Robert Townsend's message appeared. "My God!" he gasped and looked close to fainting. He swayed as he walked across to his window and opened it. The fresh air helped to revive him but it wasn't the air he wanted. It was a clear view of Anna Strong's clothes-line across the bay. There was a black petticoat fluttering there, almost invisible now that darkness was falling. He knew what that meant. "Caleb Brewster the boatman's in town," he mumbled. He strained his watery eyes to count the number of handkerchiefs on the same line. "One ... two ... three ... beached in the third bay."

This was the dangerous part. Now that the invisible message could be read he had to get it to Caleb before anyone else saw it. He pulled a cloak from a wall cupboard and shrugged his feeble body into it. He crept past the British officers' door. He was on tiptoe so they wouldn't hear him pass. He breathed again when he was past it then turned in horror as the door was pulled open. "Abraham!" a young blond-haired officer cried.

"What? What?"

"What are you doing, creeping around in the dark like a thief in the night?"

"I need a walk. Air. Fresh air. Feel faint. Need a walk! Along the cliffs."

"You need some company, Abraham, in case you fall over the edge. From the look of you it could happen!"

"No! Fine. I'm fine I am. Fresh air. I'll be fine."

The British officer slapped his back. "You take care, my friend."

"Yes. Fine. I'll take care. Good care!" and his voice was little more than a squeak.

Abraham knew that it would take him a day or two in bed to recover from this night, but he had to do this for his country. The fresh air really did make him feel a little better and he strode along the cliffs till he came to the bay where a whale-boat was pulled up on the shore. He could have probably climbed down the rough cliff path but he knew he'd never get back up. He was relieved to see the red glow and drifting sparks from Caleb Brewster's pipe as his messenger sat at the top of the cliff.

"Good evening, Caleb. A fine night for fishing."

"Aye," the broad-shouldered seaman nodded.

"Fine enough to row all the way to Connecticut."

"That's where I'm headed."

All the while Agent 722 Abraham Woodhull was looking back towards Setauket to see if he was being followed. When he was sure he was quite safe, he pulled the letter from his coat and thrust it into Caleb's huge hand. "It is very urgent, Caleb, and very important. You must get it there by morning!"

Even in the weak light from a chip of moon Abraham could see the surprise on Caleb's face. "Have I ever let you down, Abraham?"

Abraham felt a little guilt in himself and a warm pride in his colleague. "Never, Caleb, never."

"Get yourself back in the warm and don't worry, Abraham."

The little man felt a huge weight lifted off his shoulders as the boatman slid down the cliff path and he was able to return to his lodging with an empty pocket. By the next morning the message was with 321 – Colonel Benjamin Tallmadge, the American spy chief in Newport, Connecticut. Within a few hours it was in the hands of the American army commander, 711. The commander was also the general who had set up the Caleb Circle.

The general's name was George Washington.

Washington's spy, 355, had got her message through to him. It was a complicated way to send messages but it had proved safe in the past. This message, the most important that 355 had ever sent, was safe too.

Washington called his officers together. "The British are leaving New York to attack our friends the French. How can we stop them?"

"Attack New York and make the British race back to defend it," one officer suggested.

Washington nodded. "That's what we'll do."

"But we haven't enough men," someone argued.

The general gave a grim smile. "How many do we need?"

"Twelve thousand at least."

George Washington nodded. He picked up a quill and wrote quickly while his officers watched silently. "There you are. An order for 12,000 Americans to attack New York in two days' time." He passed the paper to his senior officer. "I want this message to fall into the hands of the British. I want it handed to a man the British trust. Do we have a spy in the British camp that they trust?"

"Yes, sir," Tallmadge said. "He's a farmer. They are sure he is one of them."

Washington said calmly, "I want them to think this really *is* an order coming from me."

"Then we *aren't* going to attack New York?" someone asked.

"There's no need. When the British read this they will give up the attack on the French. We will go and march to meet our allies and have a force strong enough to drive the British out." The man who had created the Culper Ring looked around at his officers. "Gentlemen, we will win this war. But we won't win it because we have the biggest army or the best weapons. We will win it because we know more about the enemy than the enemy knows about us. You soldiers will get the medals, but the real heroes will be the ones who risk their lives to spy for their country. Remember them, gentlemen. Remember them."

Washington's plan worked perfectly. The British believed his fake message and missed the chance to attack the French when they were at their weakest. Washington's Americans went on to win their fight for independence.

The men of the Culper Ring are heroes – but no one has ever discovered the name of their greatest spy. The woman, an American heroine, who will forever be known simply as 355.

The Culper story is a good example of secret ways of sending information. A vital thing for spies...

Spy Messages – FACT FILE

1. Invisible ink has been used for thousands of years and has been made from milk, vinegar, lemon juice and even urine! A World War I Belgian spy wrote an invisible ink message on the back of a woman and sent her through German defences. Sadly she was caught, the message was uncovered and she was shot.

The problem was that messages in secret inks had to be kept quite short. They are still used but have been largely replaced by radio messages and miniature photographs.

2. In 1853, French inventor Prudent Dagron used a special camera to shrink a picture of a page to a small dot. He had invented a top spy tool – the "microdot". Of course carrying the messages was a different problem. Dagron rolled a strip of 3,000 microdots into a tube and fastened it to the tail of a homing pigeon. It worked. Today a message can be reduced 40,000 times, so a 300-page book can be printed on a postage stamp.

3. One of the first people to use pigeons was Julius Caesar in 50 BC, to send reports home to

FACT NO. FILE

TOP SECRET

Rome. By World War I the birds had miniature cameras strapped to them so they could be flown over enemy defences and photograph them. In World War II British pigeons were dropped on miniature parachutes to agents in France. The agents made their reports and the pigeons took them back to Britain. German soldiers soon learned about this and had orders to shoot any suspicious looking pigeons. The heroic pigeons that did get home safely were often eaten once their message had been read!

4. In World War I a German spy used a dog to carry messages across the British trenches to his friends. It then returned with food and water to the spy's hiding-place. British soldiers saw the dog jumping the trenches every night and at first thought it was a phantom. Then the spy died and the howling dog was discovered. British Intelligence Officers tried to catch it but failed several times ... though they did trap one another in their clumsy nets. At last a soldier came up with the answer – he took a female dog along one night and the lonely spy dog couldn't resist walking into the trap.

5. Morse Code was invented in the 1840s for sending messages by telegraph or by flashing lights. It has been replaced by newer methods of sending messages and has in fact been abandoned. But for over a hundred years it was a valuable spy tool.

A French woman agent wanted to pass on a message to an English spy in a café in 1914 and didn't want to be overheard. She came up with the idea of blinking at him in Morse Code! A brilliant spy idea! Sadly the Englishman had never learned the code.

6. Opper de Blowitz was a reporter for the British newspaper, *The Times*. In 1878 he got an amazing amount of information to London about a meeting in Berlin that was supposed to be secret. One of the members of the meeting was passing information to de Blowitz. Enemy agents tailed the reporter but never caught him meeting anyone, sending letters or picking up packages from secret locations. How did he do it? Every day he and his informer went to the same restaurant for lunch – they never sat together or spoke. But they each hung up their top hat as they went in to the restaurant, and

picked up the other one's hat as they left. The enemy agents never spotted the switch.

7. A Greek called Histiaeus was imprisoned by the Persians but was allowed to send a slave with a letter to his cousin Aristagoras. The Persians read the letter but could see no code or secret meaning. The message was a perfectly harmless letter. They let the slave take the letter to Aristagoras. As soon as the slave arrived he said to Aristagoras, "Shave my head." The real message was tattooed on his scalp. This idea was still being used during World War II.

8. In World War I the Dutch and Belgians came up with some clever ideas to send messages to one another. A Belgian farmer hid them in the bodies of slaughtered pigs while another fastened them round the shaft of an arrow and shot them over the barbed wire border. A boy flew a kite over the border and snapped the string so it carried its message safely across.

9. The most gruesome Dutch messenger was a corpse. The message was hidden beneath the body in a coffin – the German border patrol did not want to search the corpse. They even gave it a guard of honour as it took its secrets through their checkpoint.

10. One of the safest World War I message-carriers was the entertainer who performed on stage as a "memory man" – he held all the messages and secrets in his head.

Or, just as safe, was the Frenchman who wrote the messages on a cigarette paper, crumpled it into a ball and hid it behind his glass eye. A German border guard was not going to say, "Take out your eye!".

FACT FILE

SET A SPY TO CATCH A SPY

*Intelligence services try to gather as much information as they can
about enemies of the state – people who want to cause trouble in their
own country as well as foreign enemies. Counter-intelligence services
try to stop enemy agents spying on them. In Russia in 1906 the
government was plagued by revolutionaries – men and women who
wanted to destroy the Tsar and his royal family, then take over the
country for themselves. But these revolutionaries were simply Russian
students and workers by day and assassins only when they needed to
be. How do you begin to look for enemies of the state when they look
just like honest people? You use a spy ...*

Date: 1906
Place: St Petersburg, Russia

The cellar below the college was dimly lit by oil lamps. They
made the stuffy room hot and smoky at the best of times. Now
it was crowded with young men and women it was like a
furnace. They murmured softly, and some looked nervously
towards the door, waiting for the St Petersburg police to burst
in and arrest them.

Ivan Aseff didn't seem to notice the heat, though the sweat
ran down from his thick, dark hair and into his eyes. He sat on
the platform with three men and a woman. Their clothes were
shabby and their faces thin and hungry, but they didn't look
like killers. Ivan rose to his feet, held up a hand and the
murmuring died.

"Brothers and sisters of the Social Revolutionary Party.
Welcome. A special welcome to the new members who have
joined us tonight. You have come here and put your lives at
risk. If the police know you belong to the party then they will
shoot you." Suddenly his dark, bearded face lightened with a
grin. "And if the party discover that you were sent by the
police ... then *we* will shoot you!"

There was a nervous laugh from the students which Ivan waved away. "You are only here because at least two friends have spoken for you. Have no fear, we trust you. We know you are here because you believe in the revolution. And you know that there is only one way to win the war against the Tsar and his evil state. By violence."

There was a lot of murmuring in agreement and nodding of heads. "Kill the lot of them," a long-haired girl with wild eyes said, and several students clapped.

"We cannot kill them all," Ivan said calmly. "But we can kill their leaders. If we remove the heads of state then it will be like removing the heads of a coop full of chickens. The bodies will collapse shortly after."

"We can't get near them," a small man in a dust-coloured jacket cried. "The Secret Police protect them too well."

Ivan Aseff opened his eyes wide and spread his hands. "Then what have we got to do first, comrade?"

The little man frowned and shook his head. Then the long-haired girl shouted, "Kill Peter Stolypin, the Secret Police chief!"

That idea was greeted by more cheers. "Thank you, Comrade Olga. We must kill that villain Stolypin, then the headless Secret Police will collapse."

"Shoot him!" someone called.

"Blow up his office!"

"Bomb his car!"

The student leader held up a hand for calm. "It is clear that a large group like this cannot make a detailed plan to assassinate Stolypin. We need to form one of our assassination squads."

"Aye, a Battle Organization," the little man said.

"Exactly, Boris, a Battle Organization. A few trusted

people who will make a plan and carry it out. If everyone in this room tries to plan then it will be hard to keep the secret. And, don't forget, there is always the chance that the police have planted a spy in the room."

Students looked nervously at one another and wondered if they could trust even their best friend.

"I want names!" Ivan said suddenly. "Names of people we trust to help me in this Battle Organization. If there are any doubts about any member, then vote against them and keep our secret safe."

Ten names were put forward and voted on. Many of the students named had enemies in the room and were voted out. After 20 minutes of arguing Ivan was left with only two names. Two people who were trusted by everyone. The wild-eyed Olga and the shabby Boris.

"This meeting will carry on with Nikita in charge," Ivan announced. "You will discuss ways of damaging the rail links between here and Moscow. Meanwhile, I will go and plan with Comrade Olga and Comrade Boris."

The three members of the Battle Organization left the steaming room and climbed the stairs to the college restaurant. "We are in full view of everyone here!" Olga objected.

"All the better," Ivan told her. "No one will suspect that we would meet to plot in a public place like this."

Little Boris nodded wisely. "We are just three friends sharing some tea."

"Now, comrades, you will divide this task between you. One must watch Minister Peter Stolypin carefully so we know his movements and can plot the best time and place to strike. The other must arrange for the assassination."

"I will carry out the assassination," Boris said. "I killed the Minister for Education back in 1901. I have proved myself. I deserve the honour of killing Stolypin."

"And I'll watch his movements," the girl said. "I have a disguise as a street flower-seller that lets me stand outside the government buildings."

"You will each need a team of helpers," Ivan Aseff told them. "Gather together the people that you trust the most. Then write down their names and addresses on a sheet of paper and give them to me in a week's time."

"Why?" Boris asked.

"What will you be doing?" Olga put in.

"I will be their guardian angel," Ivan said and sipped at his tea. "I have contacts inside the Secret Police ... friends of the Social Revolutionary Party. They will make sure that you and your teams are safe from arrest."

Boris frowned and wiped his nose on the sleeve of his faded jacket. "Why can't they kill Peter Stolypin themselves if they are so close to him?"

"Because they would give themselves away. They have other duties. Once Stolypin is dead we go for the blood of the Tsar himself. And *you*, Boris ... *you* can go down in history as the man who destroyed that wicked tyrant."

The little man seemed to grow a little at the thought. "Stolypin first, the Tsar next."

"Exactly," Ivan smiled. "Now, make your plans – and make those lists – then meet me here exactly seven days from now." Olga and Boris rose. "Remember," Ivan told them. "Do not do *anything* without telling me first. We need iron discipline. It is only with discipline that we will win through."

Ivan watched them go as he sat back and finished his tea. "The workers have nothing to lose but their chains," he muttered to himself. "They have a world to gain. Workers of the world, unite."

One week later he was sitting at the same table. Olga arrived first, her thin face wearing a broad grin and her coat flapping around her as she walked across the restaurant. "Calm, Olga, calm," Ivan muttered. "We never know who is watching and who is a spy for the government."

"But I have exciting news!" she said, pushing her long hair back from her pale face.

"Then you can tell Boris too – here he is now," Ivan said. "See the way he strolls across the room as if he were going to meet his tax inspector – not his fellow terrorists? Copy him, Olga, copy him."

"Yes, Comrade Ivan," she said humbly.

Boris sat at the table and took out a bundle of papers. "My lecture notes," he said. "See? Here are my notes on the history of Tsar Peter the Great." He pushed the papers across to Ivan and said in a low voice, "Take the bottom paper and put it in your pocket – do not let anyone see you do it. That is a list of the names of my bomb makers, the suppliers of the explosives and the fuses and so on."

"Very interesting!" Ivan said, then lowered his voice too. "Well done, Comrade Boris." He looked at Olga. "See how we do things in the Battle Organization? Trust no one, Olga. No one."

She leaned forward with a worried expression. "My list is in my pocket," she breathed.

"Then leave your coat over the back of the chair, fetch us some tea and I will take it out when I'm sure it is safe," Ivan said.

As she left the table the Battle Organization leader smiled at Boris. "She is willing, but still has a lot to learn. It seems she has news for us."

When the girl returned she could not wait to begin.

"Minister Peter Stolypin is having an official party at his villa next Thursday."

"We would never get past the security," Ivan Aseff sighed.

"Leave that to me," Boris said. "There are ways."

"What ways are those?" his leader said stiffly. "You must do nothing without my approval."

"I and three of my best men will disguise ourselves as waiters. We will enter by the kitchens and move into the main room. We will plant bombs near where Stolypin will be sitting."

Ivan nodded slowly and asked questions about the details of the attack. "And I will see my contacts in the Secret Police and make sure one of our friends is on duty at the kitchen door." He quickly smiled at his comrades. "Well done, Olga. Well done, Boris. We will not meet again before Thursday night. It will be a glorious day for the revolution."

"The Tsar next," Boris said fiercely and his fist gripped the tea cup hard.

"The Tsar next," Ivan agreed.

The leader of the Battle Organization left the college and turned towards the city of St Petersburg. The street lighting was poor. Anyone could have been following him. They would be well hidden in the deep pools of shadow and the darkened doorways but Ivan Aseff never looked back once. He passed the front of the bleak stone face of the government offices and turned down a narrow alley between two blocks. A yellow lamp burned dully over a doorway and he stepped inside.

A uniformed guard looked up from a desk and said, "Good evening, Aseff."

"Minister Stolypin is expecting me," the terrorist said politely. Five minutes later he was sitting in a deep cushioned chair in the minister's office. Stolypin sat next to him. He was a heavy man with several chins rolling over a starched white collar. His thick eyebrows went upwards and made him look like a startled devil.

"So, Ivan, who is the victim to be this time?"

Ivan Aseff gave a slow grin. "Actually, *you* are, Peter."

The minister glared at him. "That is not funny."

"The Social Revolutionary Party chose you as their chief target ... I had to go along with them."

"And you had better make sure the plot does not succeed."

"It won't!" Ivan laughed. "Not with me organizing it."

The minister took a cigar from his pocket and used it to point at the terrorist. "You set up an assassination attempt on the Minister of Education," he reminded him.

"It's the best way to bring the assassins out into the open where you can arrest them. You arrested 12 members of the Social Revolutionary Party that day."

"But that assassination attempt worked! The minister died," Stolypin cried.

"Sometimes we have to pay a small price for our success," Ivan shrugged.

"You are not paying it with my life," Stolypin said, and bit hard on the cigar.

Ivan took two sheets of paper from his pocket. "Here are the names of the plotters…"

"I'll arrest them now."

"No! If you do that they'll know they've been betrayed. You must wait till Thursday evening before you have them arrested."

"Thursday evening? That's the night of the official party at my villa."

"Exactly. Wait till then. You can net all of these fish at the same time and I can go on with the next plot."

"Which is?"

"After I've failed to kill you I am going to fail to kill the Tsar!" Ivan said cheerfully. "If I am going to be any use at all, then the Battle Organization have to believe that your clever police defeated them. They must never suspect a spy in their midst."

"Hah!" the minister laughed harshly. "You are *not* in their midst though, are you? You're at the top!"

"The top," Ivan agreed. "That's the beauty of it. I'm at the top. The very top."

Ivan Aseff sipped tea in the restaurant at the college. Olga and Boris should be under lock and key by now, he guessed.

So he was startled to see the pale-faced girl drift across the room and sit at his table. "Olga?" he said. "What has happened?"

"A most wonderful thing," she said softly.

"What? Has Boris succeeded?"

"Boris is a hero," she said. "Who would guess that little man could be so brave?"

"He's killed Stolypin?" Ivan gasped.

"No, he's killed himself."

"Tell me exactly what happened."

"It seems the Secret Police were waiting for him and his friends at the party. But he broke free and ran into the main room where the party was being held and set off his bomb. He killed 27 of the guests and even wounded Stolypin's children."

"But not Stolypin?"

"Not Stolypin."

"Thank God."

She looked at him curiously and saw something new in his sweating face. "Your friends in the Secret Police ... the ones who should have let him through ... they didn't," she said.

"Obviously."

A squad of four soldiers with rifles stopped at the door of the café and their sergeant threw it open. The girl had her back turned towards them but Ivan could see them clearly.

"Just how friendly *are* you with the Secret Police?" she asked.

The sergeant marched across the floor, his boots clattering on the bare boards.

"Very friendly," Ivan said.

"The Social Revolutionary Party will have you executed," Olga hissed as the soldier put his firm hands on her thin arms and dragged her away.

"They'll never find out," Ivan told her as she was dragged towards the door.

"I'll tell them!" she screamed.

The soldiers pulled back the bolts on their rifles and covered her with the cold steel bayonets. "No, Olga," Ivan

Aseff said. "You won't be telling anyone anything. Take her away, Sergeant."

The sergeant saluted the terrorist traitor. "Yes, sir."

When it became clear that the Revolutionaries were winning the struggle against the Royalists, Ivan Aseff simply changed sides again. He joined a plot to kill the Tsar. The plot failed, but that wasn't Aseff's fault – he really had plotted to kill his old friends' leader. Within ten years the Tsar had given up his throne. A year later the Revolutionaries shot him and his family dead.

Boris's disguise as a waiter had helped him kill several of the Tsar's supporters and, for spies, disguise has always been one of their greatest weapons...

Spying is called a "cloak and dagger" business. The truth is a spy would soon be spotted if he or she wore a cloak or a dagger! A spy will usually try to appear as someone harmless who has a perfect right to be where they are.

1. In 1582 an old man in a grey cloak was arrested as he crossed from Scotland into northern England. He claimed to be a dentist and had all the instruments for the job, so the border guards let him through. Luckily they kept his equipment. Their captain, Sir John Forster, examined the instruments closely and came across a coded message hidden behind the mirror. It was a letter from the French to Mary Queen of Scots and the discovery helped the English defeat a plot against the life of Queen Elizabeth I. Mary Queen of Scots was executed – the deadly dentist lived.

2. King Louis XV of France (1710–1774) used the agent Chevalier d'Eon as a spy. They decided that d'Eon would be best disguised as a woman. Of course, he couldn't suddenly turn up as a strange woman at a meeting with foreign visitors and talk about their secrets. They would suspect and check up on him. So he spent *years* dressed as a woman to make his disguise foolproof. At the end of his life he moved to London where he kept his identity as a woman. His British friends were shocked to discover, at his funeral, that he was a man!

3. Disguises not only help spies get into secret places, they also help them to escape if they are caught. Robert Baden-Powell acted like a harmless drunk to get into German shipyards. He was soon arrested, but the guards let him go when they *smelled* him! He had soaked his clothes in brandy and they were sure he really was an innocent drunk.

4. British spies landing in France during World War II had a problem with beach landings: boot prints in the sand as they walked up the beach from their landing boats. British "Special Operations Executive" (SOE) came up with an answer. They made rubber footprints that strapped on to the boots and left footprints in the sand. Anyone seeing them would guess it was just a swimmer … maybe. There are just two things wrong with this amazing disguise: (1) it would have been easier for agents to just take their boots off and (2) a German defender seeing the footprints may just suspect they belonged to a British Agent walking barefoot up the beach! Was it worth it?

5. Most people think of false beards and wigs as quick disguises for spies. Real spies know how difficult it is to make a false beard look natural and a beard that is clearly false will just attract attention. It is easier for them to simply shave off hair rather than try to add it. Cheek pads inside the mouth can change the shape of the face and some spies have even had surgery to alter their appearance, but that takes time, of course.

6. Spies wanting to take pictures of foreign buildings have often posed as tourists. They stood someone in front of their camera, but were really taking a picture of the building behind their friend. (Because the person in the picture was often someone's relative these pictures became known as "Aunt Minnies".) One spy was cycling alone in Austria before World War II. He made friends with the guards at a secret army camp. He asked the guards if he could have their picture to take home and they posed for him while he took photographs of the defences behind them!

BRUSH WITH DEATH

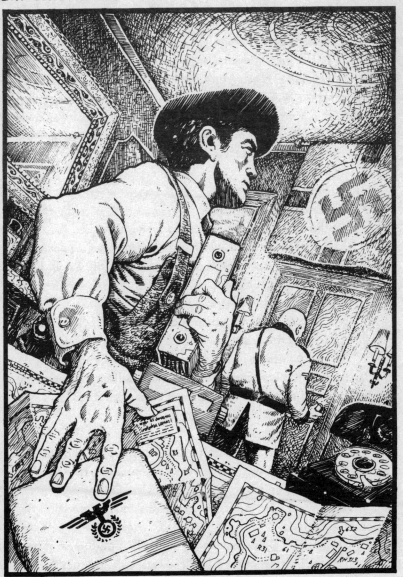

When war comes, spies are as valuable to a nation as soldiers. But spies don't have to be trained and paid agents. Sometimes the most unlikely people can show courage and cunning to outwit the enemy. In 1943 the German army had occupied much of France. Some French people tried to fight them in an organization known as the "Underground" – blowing up German road and rail links, sending reports to their British allies or helping crashed pilots to escape capture. Other French men and women simply took every chance they could to make life difficult for the Germans, even though they would have been executed without mercy if they had been caught.

Date: May 1943
Place: Caen, France

"What did you do in the war, Papa?" the boy asked.

René Duchez pushed his chair back from the supper table and picked at his teeth with a grubby fingernail. "A little of this, a little of that," he said.

"Were you a soldier?" the boy asked.

"No, Jacques. The Germans took over Caen before I had a chance to join the army."

"So, did you fight in the Underground? Michelle Simon's Papa was in the Underground. He was a fighter and they gave him a medal after the war. Did you fight with him?"

"No. I wasn't in the Underground."

"So what did you do?"

The boy's mother, Odette Duchez, came in from the kitchen to take away his plate. "He made a nuisance of himself!" she laughed.

"You smack my ear if I make a nuisance of myself," the child grumbled.

"Your father would have got a bullet behind the ear if he'd been caught," his mother said. "He was a spy, Jacques!"

The boy's eyes opened wide in wonder. "Were you really, Papa?"

Duchez spread his hands. "I did what I could."

"Tell me about it!"

"It was nothing special," the man said, pulling down the corners of his mouth, yet looking pleased at the same time.

"Come on, Duchez," his wife said. "Tell him about the time you stole the secret plans."

"Very well," the man said, and poured himself a glass of wine. "As you know, I am a decorator. Whenever I could I worked for the Germans. I hoped I could pick up bits of information once I was inside their headquarters and their camps. If I was painting a room and I overheard something, then I'd pass it on to my friends in the *Café des Touristes*. They had contacts in the Underground, of course."

"But tell me about the secret plans," young Jacques demanded.

"I'm coming to that," Duchez said. "It all started when I saw an advert in the town hall. The Germans wanted someone to decorate their commander's office. I went down to the camp to see the officer in charge. Mind you, it was hard to get in to see him. There were sentries on guard. Their French was poor and my German wasn't too good either. I tried to explain that I was a painter. I walked up to the side of the sentry box and pretended to paint it." Suddenly Duchez laughed.

"What's funny, Papa?"

"The sentry smacked me in the face with the back of his hand and knocked me off my feet!"

"Why did he do that?"

"Because the German leader, Adolf Hitler, used to be a house painter. The sentry thought I was making fun of their hero! Hah! The man dragged me to my feet and dragged me in to see his captain. Of course that's exactly the man I wanted to see in the first place. He spoke good French and at last I explained what I wanted. He said there were other decorators who had already offered to wallpaper the office. I guessed that the cheapest they could do it for would be 15,000 francs – I offered to do it for 12,000. It would cost me money, but it would get me right into the heart of the German organization."

"Weren't you scared, Papa?"

"Not at first. I was just an honest decorator doing work for the Germans. Then I met Major Schnedderer. He was a heavy man, completely bald, and on his cheek there was a scar he said he got in a duel. He was not a man to upset, I could see. As usual I acted like a simple French peasant, but all the time I was looking for my chance. When that chance came it was sooner, and greater, than I could have imagined. It was the next day in fact. I took some wallpaper pattern books into Major Schnedderer's office. He was just looking through them when he had a special parcel delivered!"

"Secret letters?" Jacques guessed.

"Maps!" his father said. "Schnedderer held them up to the window to study them and I could see they were the plans of the German defences on the coast at Normandy. It was exactly what the British and Americans needed to know if they were going to land on the French coast and defeat the Germans! Then there was a knock at the door and Schnedderer went to answer it. The maps – those top secret maps – were lying on the table in front of me. 'Take one! Take one!' a voice in my head was saying. But I knew that I'd be suspected if I tried to walk out with them under my jacket. I'd be searched, then tortured until I'd given the names of my contacts in the Underground. Then I'd be killed."

"Were you scared then?"

"Terrified! My shirt was stuck to my back with the sweat running down it. My mouth was as dry as if I were in a desert. My whole body was shaking. If that pile of plans were all copies of the same plan, then they might not miss one. If they were all different, then he would notice a missing one immediately. It was a gamble."

"So what did you do?" the boy breathed.

"I crossed the room. Schnedderer was at the door, talking to his secretary in the next room. If he just turned his head he would see me. I reached on to the table and laid my hands on the top plan. I looked around the room for somewhere to hide it. The chimney was no use. On a cold day they'd light the fire and discover it. But there was a heavy gold-framed mirror over the fireplace. I picked the map up and slipped it behind the mirror. I only hoped I'd have a chance to get it before a German discovered it."

"And did they?"

"Schnedderer came back into the room and chose his wallpaper at last. I said I'd be back on Monday to put the wallpaper up. 'I will have the walls cleared ready!' he said. 'No!' I said and I thought I was going to choke. 'That is something my workers do very well. They will put everything back exactly where they find it. There is no need for you to trouble yourself, Major!' And I walked out of the office. I don't know how. My legs would scarcely hold me up. I went straight to the *Café des Touristes* and swallowed a very large brandy, I can tell you."

Odette sat at the table next to her husband and rested her chin on her hands. "When your father told me what he'd done, I didn't sleep. He snored his great ugly head off and I lay awake. I was just waiting for the Gestapo to knock on the door, march us out and shoot us."

"Would they have shot me?" Jacques asked.

"Probably!" his mother said. "You were just a baby, but that Schnedderer may have shot you to teach the good French people of Caen a lesson!"

The boy shuddered. "But you got the plan, father."

"It wasn't that easy. I went in on the Monday morning and asked for Schnedderer. An officer called Keller said Schnedderer had been transferred! Keller was in charge now! And he was too busy sorting out his new job to have his office papered that day ... or the next day! It was going to be Wednesday before I got into the room!"

"Two more nights without sleep," Odette Duchez sighed. "You know, we had Gestapo officers living just two doors away from us. I'll swear I almost fainted every time I saw one walk past our door."

"That was nothing to the terror of walking into Keller's

office that Wednesday morning," Duchez said. "After all, he could have found the map and simply waited and watched for me to collect it. As soon as he left me alone I checked that it was still there and I took it out. But that could have been part of his plan! He'd wait till I walked out and then arrest me with the map in my bag!"

"Is that what happened?"

"I worked all day in that office. I finished at five, rolled the map up and pushed it inside my jacket pocket. I said good-night to Keller. He just nodded at me. I walked down the stairs, past guards on the door. I said good-night to them. They let me leave. Then I reached the sentries at the fence. They let me walk through. I walked straight down the main street, all the time waiting for a voice to cry 'Halt!' and order me back. Or even just a bullet in the back of the head. It seemed that hundred-metre walk to the *Café des Touristes* was a hundred kilometres! But did I lose my nerve?"

"No, Papa."

"No. I stepped through the door and my friends were waiting for me. Deschambres, the plumber, Dumis, the mechanic and Harivel, my contact in the Underground. And at the table nearest the counter was a German soldier."

"To arrest you?" Jacques gasped.

"He *could* have been. He was an old soldier who often called in to the *Café des Touristes* when his duty was finished for the day. We thought he was a spy at first, but soon learned he was quite harmless. His army overcoat was hanging by the door and I pushed my way past it to get to the table of my friends. 'Well?' they asked. 'I have it,' I said quietly, though we knew old Albert could speak no French."

"But he would have seen you hand over the map!" Jacques said.

"He *would* have seen me hand over the map. So I *didn't*! Imagine the danger! There was a police car outside the café with two men in raincoats seated in the back. I knew they were not French police – they were German Secret State Police, the Gestapo. They could have come in at any time to search us."

"You had to get out of there quickly!" René's son said.

"It would have done no good. They could have stopped me just as easily outside!"

"So what did you do?"

"I played dominoes with my friends, of course. And I kept playing until the car with the Gestapo started up, drove slowly past the café and then disappeared out of the town."

"Then you handed over the map?"

"There was *still* old Albert inside the café, remember."

"Of course."

"Then Albert finished his drink and got up to go. I jumped to my feet, stepped across to the door and took hold of his overcoat. When he reached the coat-stand, I held up the coat and helped him to get into it. 'Danke schön,' he said – that is German for 'Thank you'. And he left! Harivel asked, 'What have you got for me? There is one more train to Paris today. I can be on it if you have important information.' And I told him, 'The *most* important information you will ever carry!' And I took the plans from inside my jacket. He was on the train to Paris and the plans were with the British inside a week."

"That was dangerous!" young Jacques said. "What if the Gestapo had come into the café and searched you?"

René Duchez grinned and looked at his wife. "If they had searched me from head to toe they would have found absolutely nothing!"

"Was it magic?" Jacques asked.

"No."

"Were they hidden under the table?"

"No."

"Then what did you do with them?" the boy cried.

"What would *you* have done with them?" his father asked.

"Stop teasing him and tell the lad," Odette said.

René Duchez sat back in his chair and took a long drink of the red wine. "I hid them in the only safe place in the whole café. I hid them in the overcoat pocket of old Albert, the German soldier!"

"You didn't!"

"As I entered the café I'd seen the Gestapo car and I didn't want to be caught with the plans. I certainly didn't want to pass them over to Harivel for *him* to get caught. I slipped them into the soldier's coat when it was hanging on the coat-stand. As soon as he got up to go I grabbed the coat and took them out again. *He* thought I was being a gentleman. *I* knew I was helping to defeat him and his invaders."

Jacques eyes were glowing. "Wait till I tell Michelle Simon! My father is a hero!"

"Germany isn't the only country to have a house painter for a hero," René shrugged.

"Did you get a medal, Papa?"

"No, my son. But when the war was over we had a great celebration in the town hall. The fighting men of the Underground were honoured – and it was only right that they should be. But when the speeches were all over and the cheering had died down, the mayor came over to me and spoke to me. 'We will never forget the part you played, René,' he said."

Madame Duchez poked him sharply in the shoulder and

said, "Tell Jacques what else the mayor said to you."

"The mayor said, 'René, there is no doubt about your madness … and there is no doubt about your courage.'"

"You see, Jacques?" Odette Duchez said as she put an arm around her husband's shoulders and squeezed. "You don't have to be a soldier with a medal to be a hero."

The secret plans that Duchez stole were vital for British and American forces when they invaded the French coast in 1944. They knew where the German defences were strong and where they were weak. They let false information reach the German defenders. It said that the British and Americans would land in one place when in fact they planned to land in another. Spies need to use such tricks to confuse an enemy…

1. Before the British and Americans landed in Italy they "accidentally" lost a secret message that showed plans to attack through Greece and Sardinia. (The truth is they meant to go through Sicily.) The secret message was planted on a dead body and dropped into the Mediterranean Sea for the Germans to find. The corpse was given a completely fake identity, as "Major Martin". His pockets held bills, theatre tickets and love-letters – all faked – as well as the secret plans for the phoney Greece plan. The Germans fell for the trick and rushed to defend Greece while their enemies landed in Sicily. The real name of the dead man is still a secret – he is simply known as "The man who never was".

2. The "man who never was" story is famous. Not so many people know a similar idea had been tried in World War I. A British officer rode past Turkish defences and was fired at. He dropped the haversack he was carrying and appeared to have been hit. He tried to go back for it but was driven off by rifle fire and the Turks captured the bag. It was soaked in fresh blood and had a British plan of attack inside.

FACT FILE

The British let the Turks overhear radio messages saying how desperate they were to get the sack safely returned. Of course the plans were false and the blood was from a slaughtered pig, but the trick worked and sent the Turk defenders in the wrong direction.

3. If a spy is captured then it is vital that messages should be destroyed. British spy, Robert Baden-Powell, was held in an Austrian jail when the local police suspected him of spying. While they waited for their intelligence agents to arrive they kindly allowed Baden-Powell to roll some cigarettes and smoke them. Of course his spy notes were written on the cigarette papers and he destroyed them. (Baden-Powell described this trick in a popular book he wrote. Later spies, who were foolish enough to try the same thing, were usually caught and often executed. Smoking can damage your health!)

4. During World War II spies were dropped into enemy countries by parachute and then had to bury the parachutes. But the German airforce sometimes dropped empty parachutes to make the British *think* there were spies everywhere and to waste police and Home Guard time in looking for them.

5. Spies who want to pass on messages need a "letter-box" – not a hole in somebody's door, but simply a safe place to leave a message for a partner to collect. A "live letter-box" is a person who will hold the message for you and a "dead letter-box" (or a "dead drop") is just an agreed place. A dead letter-box can be a hollow tree, a hole in the ground or the boot of a parked car. Anywhere that a message can be hidden in fact.

6. During World War II the Germans took over a cottage owned by an old French woman. Their maps were all over the walls but were guarded, even at night. The old woman contacted the local Resistance agent and told him to come with a camera. She gave the guard coffee full of herbs that gave him diarrhoea. Every time the guard trotted off to the toilet at the bottom of the garden the agent slipped in and photographed the maps!

THE APPLE SPY

By the start of World War II, the Scots found they agreed with the English over one matter; they didn't like Mister Hitler and his Nazi bully boys. They fought shoulder to shoulder with their old enemy to defeat the new enemy, Germany.

Everyone remembers the "Blitz" over London. But Scotland produced a lot of warships and weapons, so she got her share of German bombs.

Scotland was also a good place to land a German spy. There were miles of deserted coastline where secret agents could be landed without being spotted. In September 1940 a group of three almost got away with it. The sharp wits of a few Scots – and a bit of luck – saved Britain from danger...

Date: September 1940
Place: Portgordon and Edinburgh, Scotland

Detective Superintendent William Merrilees stood with his back to a map of Edinburgh and spoke quietly but quickly to the men and women crowded into the room. "Two foreigners arrived at Portgordon railway station at 7:30 this morning, a man and a woman. Stationmaster John Donald became suspicious when the woman asked the name of the station. Of course, all signs have been taken down because of the war. The man pointed to the timetable on the wall and asked for two tickets to Forres. The stationmaster noticed that the man's wallet was crammed with English pound notes. He also noticed that the bottom of the man's trousers were soaked and so were the woman's stockings. He told porter John Geddes to keep the couple talking while he telephoned Constable Grieve at the local police station."

The uniformed police in the room looked grim. Constable Nixon, who always fancied himself as the Sherlock Holmes of the Lothian and Borders Police Force, turned to Policewoman

Ellen Johnston on his left. "Holiday-makers, mark my words," he murmured. "Caught by the tide."

"Really?" she gasped, wide-eyed. "What would they be doing on the north-east coast?"

"Fishing," Constable Nixon said with a wise wink.

Superintendent Merrilees went on, "They were, of course, spies."

Constable Nixon coughed quietly. "I thought so. Spies pretending to be holiday-makers."

Merrilees went on, "Constable Grieve ran from his office to the railway station and asked to see the couple's identity papers. The man and woman claimed to be refugees, but their papers had no stamp to show where they had entered Britain. And both cards were in a continental style of handwriting."

"Tut! Tut! Tut!" Nixon clucked. "I'd have spotted that at once."

"Grieve phoned his superintendent at Buckie and the couple were searched. Apart from over £300 in banknotes, they were carrying a Mauser pistol and ammunition, a wireless transmitter and a code book. But the real give-away was the piece of German sausage they were carrying. No one has been able to buy such a sausage in Scotland since the war started."

"Never liked the stuff much anyway," Nixon sniffed.

"A close search in the Portgordon and Buckie area revealed that a third spy had taken a train to Edinburgh. He arrived here at 4:30 this afternoon."

There was a stir of excitement among the police in the room. Nixon looked at his watch. "Forty-five minutes ago. He could be anywhere by now."

"We'll comb the city," Superintendent Merrilees ordered and began to give tasks to small teams of men and women. Some were to try the hotels, others were to look in the cinemas and a large group was to search the railway yards near the station. He looked at Nixon and Policewoman Ellen Johnston. "You two can come with me."

Nixon inflated his chest. "That's because we're the cream," he smiled.

"No," the superintendent frowned. "I was just thinking that if the German shot you, then Edinburgh Police wouldn't be losing much!"

"What?"

"A joke, Nixon. Just my little joke. Now, let's get down to the station and see what we can find out."

The three officers arrived at the great gloomy Waverley Station and marched to the stationmaster's office. A shrivelled old porter stood there, twisting his battered cap between his fingers. "You're McGregor?" Superintendent Merrilees asked.

"Yes, sir."

"And you helped this foreign gentleman when he stepped off the Aberdeen train?"

"I did, sir."

"Tell us exactly what happened."

"He stepped down with his case and asked if this was Edinburgh. I said, 'Well it's not New York!' He didn't laugh. He just asked where he'd get the London train and I said Platform 6. Then he asked what time, and I said 10:00 p.m. tonight. He looked a bit upset at that."

"He left the station, did he?"

"Aye, sir. Headed up to Princes Street."

"In a brown overcoat and black felt hat. Age about 30 you said?"

"That's right, sir."

Merrilees shook his head. "He'll be hard to spot in the crowds."

"What about the case?" Policewoman Johnston asked quietly.

The superintendent clicked his fingers. "Good thought, Johnston. What sort of case was he carrying?"

"He wasn't," McGregor said.

"You told us he stepped off the train with a case," Merrilees said sharply.

The old porter looked sly. "I *did*. But he put it in the Left Luggage office, didn't he!"

"Why didn't you say so?" the police chief snapped.

"You never asked."

Two minutes later the three officers were examining a large suitcase. "Do you think this is the one?" Merrilees asked.

"There's a white stain on it," Policewoman Johnston pointed out. "Probably sea water."

The senior officer looked at her with admiration. "Well done, Ellen. I'm glad we brought you along."

"I noticed that stain," PC Nixon whispered to the policewoman.

"Let's just force it open, shall we? Here we go ... what have we here?"

"A radio, sir," Nixon said quickly before Ellen could identify the metal box with dials.

"A *German* radio, Nixon. Very important. And two apples! We know what they'll be for."

"To eat?" Nixon nodded wisely.

"But you see what's missing?" the superintendent asked.

"A gun, sir," Ellen Johnston said.

"That's good!" Constable Nixon said brightly.

"That's *bad*, Nixon," Merrilees said with a shake of the head.

"Very bad," the policewoman agreed.

Nixon looked at her blankly. She explained. "He's sure to have a gun, but he must have it with him. That makes it dangerous for anyone who tries to arrest him."

The constable swallowed hard. "Yes. I was thinking that."

His senior officer slapped him on the back. "Sorry, Nixon, I know you'd like the glory of the arrest yourself. But it's so risky I just can't ask another man to do it. I'll arrest him myself."

Constable Nixon breathed out slowly. "If you insist, sir."

"Never mind," Ellen said squeezing his arm. "You'll have your chance to show your bravery another day."

"I will," the policeman nodded.

They laid their plan carefully and by eight o'clock they were in position. Superintendent Merrilees was dressed in a porter's uniform and standing behind the desk of the Left Luggage office. Constables Nixon and Johnston stood in the shadows. The evening grew darker and there were only a few dim lights in the station, and none in the blacked-out city outside. The smoke of the trains smelled sharp and stung their nostrils. Trapped in the canopy of the station it formed a thin, sooty mist.

Nine o'clock rang on the clock of the Balmoral Hotel and a man in a black hat walked quickly up to the Left Luggage counter. "Evening, sir!" Merrilees said brightly.

The man didn't reply but pushed a slip of paper over the counter.

"Number two-seven-three, sir?" the police officer said. He brought the case to the counter and noticed that the stranger kept his right hand in his pocket. "Hang on a moment, sir, and I'll bring it round the counter to you."

He raised a flap in the counter and heaved the case through. The stranger reached out a left hand but kept his right hand in his pocket. "Here, sir, I'll call a porter for you," the superintendent said quickly. He looked across the dim alley that led to the platforms and shouted, "Nixon!"

The stranger turned away, as Merrilees knew he would. In an instant the superintendent let go of the case and grabbed the man's right arm. The stranger struggled but Nixon was running towards them with Policewoman Johnston. Together they forced the hand out of the overcoat pocket and saw the man was indeed holding a gun.

"I arrest you on suspicion of espionage against His Majesty King George's government," Nixon said with a wide grin to Ellen Johnston.

She nodded with satisfaction.

That evening they were in the canteen at the central police station telling the story of the spy for the 20th time. Each time the struggle was longer and Nixon's heroism greater.

A message arrived at the table where they were drinking tea. "The prisoner is asking to speak to the brave officer that arrested him."

Nixon rose to his feet. "I guess he's ready to confess. He knows he's met his match with me."

"Can I come with you?" Ellen Johnston asked.

"Of course you can, Ellen. See a bit of good policing in action."

They walked through the police station, down the shabby green corridors until they came to the cell that held the man. The prisoner clutched at the bars, his dark eyes staring and pleading. "My apples," he said. "You have my apples?"

"I have," Nixon said.

"May I have them. Please?"

"I came to hear you confess, not to run errands for you."

"Ah!" the man nodded. "Fetch my apples and I will tell you everything. The codes, the drop-off points, the names of agents already in your country. The whole of the German spy network. Anything."

Nixon could see his name in the newspaper headlines. "I'll get a notepad and pencil."

"And the apples?"

"And the apples."

The spy gave a slow smile. "I knew you would help me."

Nixon turned and walked back towards the main office. "I wonder where we can find two wrinkled apples at this time of night?" Ellen asked.

"What for?"

"To give him," Ellen said.

"Give him his own apples," Nixon shrugged. "Can't be any harm in that." He reached into the suitcase and took the fruit out.

The policewoman's eyes opened wide. "Oh, but you can't do that!"

Nixon frowned. "Why not?"

"Because they're sure to be poisoned. One bite and he'll be dead. You won't get a word out of him. In fact, you'll be in dead trouble!"

The constable felt suddenly faint and dropped the apples on to the top of a desk. He wiped his hands on his trousers. "Poisoned?"

"Poisoned. All spies carry poison with them."

He cleared his throat. "Yes, well spotted, Policewoman Johnston. I wondered how long it would take you to work that out. I knew it all along."

"Of course you did, Constable Nixon," she smiled. "Of course you did. As long as we have policemen like you, the Germans will never defeat us."

The constable poked at the apples with a finger. "Hah! Apples! The oldest trick in the book. Never fooled me for a minute."

He turned and collected his helmet from a rack on the wall. Only Ellen Johnston noticed that his hands were trembling as he put it on.

The three spies were taken to London for questioning and tried at the Old Bailey. All three were found guilty. The Edinburgh spy and the man caught at Portgordon were hanged. The woman was pardoned, even though it was clear she was the leader. It seems she agreed to betray her German masters and work for the British Secret Service.

She said that the three spies landed in a seaplane then rowed ashore in a dinghy. Three bicycles were lowered into the dinghy but dropped into the sea. The spies had expected to cycle 600 miles to London! If it hadn't been for the accident with the cycles, and the sharp-witted people of Portgordon and Buckie, Britain could have been in great danger. (Though a World War I spy arrived in England with his cycle and was arrested before he had ridden a quarter of a mile — he was riding on the right-hand side of the road as he always did in Germany!)

The clever Portgordon stationmaster, John Donald, was made an

MBE while Superintendent William Merrilees went on to be Chief Constable of the Lothian and Borders Police Force.

The Germans were betrayed by the radio they carried. Many spies need special equipment...

Spy Equipment – FACT FILE

The American spy organization, the Central Intelligence Agency (CIA), nicknames spy gadgets as "sneakies". But these have been around longer than the CIA.

1. Secret compartments. Hiding messages, plans and equipment from the enemy needs some careful planning. A messenger from Charles I's queen was captured by Oliver Cromwell in the English Civil War. He was stripped and searched but no message was found. It was only when Cromwell ordered his saddle to be torn apart that the vital letter was found.

2. Secret pockets. In the 1890s a British officer spying on a demonstration of a new exploding bullet in France had a secret pocket in the long tail of his coat. He popped the shell case into the pocket – sadly the metal was still hot and his coat-tails began to smoke and gave the game away!

3. Maps. Spies in World War II needed maps but would be shot if they were caught with one

F A C T F I L E

in their pocket. So maps were cut into 52 pieces and each piece sandwiched into a playing card. When the agent was safely out of sight he or she could peel off the face of the card and put the 52 pieces together to assemble the map again.

4. Bugs. Spies who want to listen in on enemy meetings will try to leave a microphone and transmitter in the meeting place – a "bug". These bugs are so small they can be hidden in a watch or a pen. The latest ones are just four mm thick and the size of a credit card so they can be easily hidden in a diary or a pocket calculator.

5. Cameras. Spies have wanted to photograph documents, enemy agents and secret defences ever since the camera was invented in the 1840s. By the 1880s there were cameras designed to fit into hats, ties and books. By 1948 a camera could be fitted into a wrist-watch. Modern video cameras can spy through a hole the size of a pinhead.

6. Guns. Guns need to be well hidden and Secret Service scientists have come up with many clever ones – pens and pencils that fire a shot, a ring that hid a five-shot revolver and a glove that held a single-shot pistol. Even a harmless-looking umbrella has had a gas-injector in the tip that fired a poison pellet into the victim. A Bulgarian, Georgi Markov, died from a poison umbrella shot when walking in a London street in 1978.

7. Knives. These can take the form of sharpened coins and special blades built into the heel of a shoe. Useful if the agent is tied up and needs to cut himself or herself free.

8. Bombs. A German scientist called Scheele invented a fire-bomb for use by agents in World War I. The lead tube, the size of a cigar, had two compartments separated by a thin piece of copper. One compartment held sulphuric acid and the other picric acid. The sulphuric acid ate through the copper in a few days and let the two acids mix; this created a fierce flame. If the "cigar bomb" was slipped into a bale of material or a sack of grain before it was loaded on to a ship, then a fire would start when the ship was at sea and destroy it. Doctor Scheele also

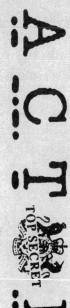

invented a fire-bomb that looked like a lump of coal and would never be noticed on a coal ship – till it went off, of course.

9. Poison pills. Many spies in World War II were given small poison pills. If they were captured then they could crush the pill between their teeth, swallow the poison and die. This would save them from being tortured and betraying their friends. Several German spies used the poison pills but there's no record of a British spy ever using one. A German spy called Hermann Goertz was imprisoned in Ireland for his spying. At the end of the war he was released and ordered to return to Germany. He believed Germany was still run by the Nazis and he'd be shot when he landed, so he took the poison and killed himself. In fact he would have been perfectly safe.

10. Poison gases. Spies in films seem to have supplies of special gases – one squirt in the face and an enemy is dead. In fact, such gases *do* exist and no doctor could tell how the victim has died – with a tiny amount you can commit the perfect murder. British and American agents say that the gas, known as FEA, has already been used by the Russians to put "problem" people out of the way.

What would you do if you were a spy and you were caught? The American spy Nathan Hale was captured by the British and told he would be executed. "I'm sorry that I have only the one life to give for my country," he said. He was hanged and became an American hero.

Before the start of World War I in 1914, spies tried to behave like gentlemen. When Colonel Alfred Redl betrayed Austria to the Russians and was caught in 1913, he asked his captors if he could have a few minutes alone. They agreed, even though they knew what he planned to do – he went to his room and shot himself. Were all spies that determined to die for their country?

Date: 17 September 1940
Place: Cambridge, England

Call me a coward and a traitor if you like. But I did *not* want to die for Germany! So why did I agree to spy for them back in 1939, you ask? For the excitement. For the *adventure*. And because it was better than being in the army with all that parading and marching and hard work.

I couldn't face joining the German army when the war started. I didn't fancy being shouted at by some red-faced, foul-mouthed sergeant. So, when the German Military Intelligence officer came to me in September 1939, I jumped at the chance to spy for them. Hah! Jumped at the chance. That's a joke! I really *did* jump – out of a plane on my first and last spying mission.

"You speak good English," the Intelligence officer said.

"I've travelled around the world," I admitted.

"We need men like you, Wulf Schmidt, to spy for us. We would train you, of course."

And the training took a year. Learning how to operate a radio, the codes I'd need and my cover story. The story was that I was Harry Williamson from Denmark – that was easy enough for me because I was born on the border with Denmark and I knew it well.

The truth was I was Agent A3725.

Then I was told I'd be sent to England to spy on their defences and their war plans. "Where will I be landed?" I asked.

"Cambridgeshire," my German instructor told me.

I laughed. "How will a submarine drop me in Cambridgeshire?"

"You are not going by submarine," he said. He was not laughing. "You will be dropped by parachute."

Have you ever jumped into a cold swimming pool and felt the shock? That was how the news chilled me. "I'm scared of heights!" I said.

"You'll be on the ground in no time," he snapped.

"That's what terrifies me!" I said.

"We drop agents on moonless nights, so you won't even see the ground."

"How will I know when I'm there?"

"You'll know," he said and he gave a yellow-toothed grin. He was enjoying this.

The parachute training was a nightmare. Sitting in the doorway at 10,000 feet and waiting to jump made me sick. Vomiting at 300 kilometres per hour is not funny. At least I wasn't afraid of being caught as a spy. "I'm not worried about what the British will do to me," I wrote and told my mother. "The parachute drop will kill me before they even get their hands on me!"

The night of the landing, 17 September 1940, was *not* so bad as I had feared – it was at least ten times *worse*. "There's a full moon!" I cried. "What happened to the idea of dropping me in the dark?"

"The bombers can see the British cities better on a moonlit night."

"I'm going to *spy* on them, not *bomb* them," I sighed.

"Your plane will cross the English Channel with a squadron of bombers. That way they won't spot your plane."

The Cambridgeshire countryside was silver-green with black shadows of hedgerows and bright ribbons of road. It was quite beautiful. It was also a long way down. I sat in the open door. "Go!" the navigator called.

At that moment the plane rocked and I was thrown against the door frame. My watch strap caught in the door latch and was ripped off my wrist. It had been a present from my mother. It spun down towards the English soil and I followed it moments later. My hand was damaged too, but I hadn't time to worry about it then. The parachute snapped open and the jerk seemed to squeeze the air from my lungs. The cold wind stung my eyes to tears and by the time I had cleared them I saw the ground was rushing towards me. Luckily, the field was soft and muddy so I managed to land without breaking my neck.

I lay on the ground and groaned for five minutes. In training they said I had to move quickly after I landed. But the trainers weren't there. I dragged myself to a ditch at the edge of the field and buried my flying suit and parachute as well as I could with my one good hand. Then I picked up my suitcase and limped on to the road.

I had seen a cluster of houses just before I dropped and set off in what seemed the right direction. For once I was in luck. The village was there, quiet in the moonlight. The village sign had been removed so that German spies would not know where they had landed. That wasn't very sporting.

I walked to the middle of the green. No lights showed from

the blacked-out windows and no one was on the streets at this late hour. I soaked my throbbing hand under the village pump and then rested my back against it. After all the tension, and a week of sleepless nights, I fell asleep. It may sound amazing, but I slept soundly under the village pump until morning.

When I woke people were passing me in the street and looking at me with suspicion. I jumped to my feet, grabbed my suitcase and brushed the creases from my suit. "Good morning!" I called to a boy with a school-bag on his back. His eyes opened wide as saucers, before he turned and ran.

Then two old men in khaki battledress uniforms shuffled towards me with ancient rifles pointing at me. The lettering on their shoulders said LDV – Local Defence Volunteers by name, but better known to the English as Dad's Army.

"Raise your hands!" one croaked. He looked more afraid than I was.

"I am a Danish businessman," I began.

"And I'm Winston Churchill," his friend sneered.

I stretched out a hand. "Pleased to meet you, Mister Churchill!" I said. He jumped back as if my hand held a gun.

"I think you had better come with us," the first one said.

My career as a spy had lasted a few hours and would last just a few hours more, I guessed. I hoped they would shoot me quickly. I couldn't face being tortured. I had already decided that if they started pushing splinters of wood up my fingernails I would talk.

The cell I was locked in was comfortable enough. The policeman in charge was even friendly. "The gentlemen from Military Intelligence will be with you in half an hour," he smiled. "Here's a cup of tea and some toast. Bet it's better than the stuff they feed you in Germany."

"I'm from Denmark!" I said.

He raised one eyebrow and laughed. "Oh yes? And I'm Winston Churchill."

"So! There are two of you in one village!" I sighed. "Amazing!"

"What's that?"

"Nothing, just my little joke."

The man who arrived to question me was small, round-faced and wearing wire-rimmed glasses. He came into the cell smoking a pipe and offered me a cigarette. "Good morning, A3725. Welcome to England!" he said.

"I am a Danish citizen," I said. "The Danish are your friends. Why do you lock me away like this?"

"You are Agent A3725 and we've been expecting you," he said and sat down with a brown folder full of papers. "Let's see," he said taking a paper out. "Two of your men landed here six months ago and your job is to make contact with them."

"I am a Danish citizen," I said.

I waited for him to tell me he was Winston Churchill too! But he just shook his head sadly. "The game's up, Wulf Schmidt."

"My name is Harry Williamson."

"Your name is Wulf Schmidt and you are here to collect information on the British war effort." He was very calm about it.

"You will torture me?" I asked.

He looked shocked. "Good lord, no! Nothing so messy as that!"

"You will shoot me, then?"

"Not unless I have to," he said with a shrug. "You are much more useful to us alive."

"Useful? To you? In what way?"

"You can send messages back to your masters in Germany."

"What sort of messages?"

"The information that they want, of course. Your two friends are already doing it for us. We caught them when they landed six months ago and they're working for us now. That's how we know all about you," he explained. "They didn't want to be shot, you see. Do you?"

"No!" I said quickly. "But I don't understand why you want me to send your secrets back to Germany."

"Because you will be telling the Germans everything *we* want them to know."

"Lies?"

"Not all of them." He took off his glasses and polished them on a huge white handkerchief. "The information is put together by a special committee called Committee 20. Now, as you know, '20' in Roman numerals is XX. It's a little joke among us – we call it 'Double Cross'. Get it? XX – double-cross."

"Very funny," I said, but I didn't laugh.

"You're right," he sighed. "Not one of the best jokes in the world. But the fact is, that's what we want *you* to do. Double-cross your German masters. We'll pay you well, look after you ... and let you live. All you have to do is feed Committee 20 information to your old friends."

"I see," I nodded. "This information will mislead the German army?"

"Exactly!" he chuckled. "And they will ask you to find certain pieces of information that will prove useful to us."

"What do you mean?"

He leaned forward. "They may ask you to take a trip north and report on anti-aircraft guns in Newcastle. What does that tell us?"

"That they are planning to bomb Newcastle?" I guessed.

"Exactly! Sometimes you will say the British have no guns there when we will really have extra ones in place. We'll blow the Luftwaffe out of the sky. Other times you will say there are a thousand guns and planes defending the place, when there aren't ... that way they may simply leave us alone. You see the way it works?"

"I see."

"Now, old chap. Do you fancy working for us? Or shall I just take you out into the yard and put a bullet in the back of your head?" he asked. He was like a kindly schoolmaster asking if I wanted to choose between playing soccer or rugby!

What do you think I said? What would *you* have said to an offer like that? Of course I said, "Yes."

"Then you will need a code name. What is it to be?" he asked and seemed to be enjoying himself.

"I called myself Harry Williamson," I told him.

"You know," he said, "we have a comedian who is very

popular in Britain. They call him Harry, too. Harry Tate. That's what we'll call you … Tate!"

So, for the next five years my friends called me Wulf, and my employers called me Tate. I was one of the best agents the Germans had in Britain. I blew up more bridges and arms factories than the Luftwaffe bombs … at least that's what my reports said.

Adolf Hitler himself was impressed by my work. In fact, the German high command believed I was such a German hero they awarded me the Iron Cross (second class and first class), their highest honours. Their radio message went on to say, "The crosses will be presented to your brother until the day you return to Germany after we have won the war."

Of course, Germany lost the war. Every single spy landed in Britain had been captured. The brave ones refused to work with the British and they were shot. But 120 of them, including me, were "turned" and used against our homeland. No wonder Germany lost the war. Every piece of spy information they received was sent by their enemy.

I couldn't keep the Iron Crosses, of course. But I did go back to my home to collect them from my brother. I went through the blackened rubble of all those ruined German towns and knew that I was in some way to blame. You have to remember, though, I had also seen the fire-storms that lit up London and the Blitz that shattered so many other British towns.

Call me a traitor, but don't blame me. Blame war.

I became a spy because I wanted excitement. I returned from the ruins of Germany with my Iron Crosses and I had had a bellyful of excitement. Enough to last me a lifetime.

The British were good to me. They said I could keep on working for them. Their old allies, the Russians, were building a wall of secrecy to keep the British and Americans out – an "Iron Curtain" Winston Churchill called it. They said I could go back to Germany to spy on the Russians. I said, "Thank you – but no." Still, the British let me stay.

I took a job as a newspaper photographer and the most excitement I've had since is a big wedding!

And somewhere, filed away and forgotten in a British Military Intelligence office, there are two of the most curious souvenirs ever to be held by one of their agents. Two German Iron Crosses for gallantry. If you will excuse the bad joke – a sort of double-cross!

Wulf Schmidt kept his wartime secret for 50 years. In 1990, a television programme was made about Committee 20 and Wulf described his work. His friends and family were astonished to learn of his spy past.

The Double Cross plan worked perfectly and the Germans never knew that their spies had died or switched sides. They continued to send messages in code, but as the British knew all their codes they may as well have sent them in clear English!

From the earliest times spies have tried to disguise their messages so that they stayed secret even if an enemy came across them...

There is always a danger that an enemy will find your message. If they do then it is probably important that they can't make any sense of it. Or at least it will slow them down. (An Arab in the 1600s decoded a message to the Sultan of Morocco, but it took him 16 years!) Since the earliest days of spying, agents have used "codes".

1. The first code-makers we know about were the Chinese of 1000 BC. Army commanders learned 40 lines of a poem. Each line meant something different. If they sent line 17, say, then it might mean, "Please send more arrows", or line 32 might mean, "I have defeated an enemy attack". The line of the poem was then included in an ordinary report so it would be impossible for an enemy to understand.

2. Alexander the Great could read his enemies' letters because they didn't use a code. He was much more careful. He wrote messages on a strip of paper spiralled round a stick. When the paper was unwound the letters were scrambled. A reader with the right sized stick could wind the paper round it and see the message again.

3. A hundred years later the Greek writer, Polybius (203–120 BC), came up with the number square. Twenty-five letters of the alphabet were arranged into five rows of five columns.

	1	2	3	4	5
1	G	Q	B	T	O
2	D	N	L	X	J
3	R	A	W	F	Y/Z
4	E	V	P	S	I
5	K	U	M	C	H

So "A" is 2 across – 3 down or 23. "B" is 31 and "D" is 12. So 31-23-12 spells "bad".

Amazingly this type of code was still being used by the French Resistance in World War II, 2,000 years later.

4. Julius Caesar used the simple trick of moving all the letters of the alphabet three spaces along. If he wanted to write ABCDE then his code said DEFGH. It is still known as the "Caesar Alphabet".

5. Mary Queen of Scots sent and received messages in prison that were hidden in beer barrels. To be extra safe she wrote letters to her agents in a code that was a mixture of Greek letters and shapes. The English spy-master, Sir Francis Walsingham, had spies who copied every letter in the barrels before they were replaced and passed on. He had a code-breaker called Thomas Phelippes who broke the code easily. Mary's agents were arrested and died horribly, half-hanged, then cut apart before being beheaded. Mary herself was beheaded shortly afterwards. All because her code was cracked.

6. In World War I, Britain and France were struggling against the German army. President Woodrow Wilson and the American people did not want to get mixed up in the battles in Europe. Then the Germans sent a coded message to their agent in Mexico. It told the Mexicans that if they invaded America from the south, then Germany would help them. The British spy-master Reginald Hall (nicknamed "Blinker" Hall because of his habit of blinking) got a copy of the message. His code-cracking expert, Reverend William Montgomery, was a schoolteacher interested in puzzles. He decoded the German message. The American people were so furious when they read the decoded message they changed their minds and America joined the war. That one broken code probably changed the course of history.

7. Two Dutch sailors in Portsmouth spied for Germany in World War I. Instead of sending a code of scrambled letters they posed as cigar salesmen and sent orders openly through the telegraph system. "1,000 Havana cigars" meant

F·A·C·T F·I·L·E

one battleship had arrived in Portsmouth harbour – "2,000 Corona cigars" meant *two cruisers* were in port. It seemed a perfect system. But a Post Office clerk noticed the size of the orders which were adding up to almost 5,000 cigars a day. The whole of Portsmouth couldn't smoke that many. British Military Intelligence Department 5 (M.I.5) arrested the men.

8. A French woman was able to send messages to spies across the valley from her house, using her washing line. She hung out garments that spelled out the message. Her ABC used the English language to confuse the Germans even further and it read as follows: Apron, Blouse, Collar, Duster, Eiderdown, Frock, Gloves, Handkerchief, Jacket, Knickers, Lace, Mat, Nightdress, Overall, Pants, Quilt, Roller-towel, Skirt, Trousers, Undershirt, Vest, Waistcoat, Yoke.

9. A World War II US general at army headquarters didn't bother sending orders in code. Instead he told a Navaho Indian on his staff the message. The Native American passed the message on to one of his tribe in the battalion who changed it back into the English instructions for the fighting men. Apart from the Navahos there were just 28 people in the world who spoke the language – and none of them was German. In the 1960s Irish troops fighting for the United Nations in the Congo spoke to one another in their native Gaelic – quite sure that no African spies could understand a word.

10. The German code machine called "Enigma" was so good at scrambling messages they believed it was completely safe. In fact one of the workers in a factory that made the Enigma machine gave the secret to the British. British experts then invented a very early sort of computer to decode "Enigma" messages and were able to read some of Germany's greatest war secrets. The Germans didn't know that their Enigma code system had been cracked and the British told no one until 25 years after the war had ended.

Spies have always used the latest inventions to keep ahead of the enemy: when cameras were invented, spies had miniature ones made; when radio came along, they were glad of a new way of reporting back to headquarters; aeroplanes became spy-planes and satellites became their eyes in the sky. At the end of this century computers hold the world's secrets. Will spies turn to using computers to search out secrets? Of course they will. What's more, they already have been for some years. Spying by computer may seem clean and safe compared to the ways of the old agents. One of the first cases to be uncovered was in Germany – it turned out to be anything but safe for one of the new breed of young spies...

Date: Autumn/winter 1989
Place: Hanover, Germany

Karl was my friend but now Karl is dead. They said he was a spy and that's why he's dead. But it wasn't that simple.

I was 14 years old in 1986. Most boys in my class were interested in football – a few were interested in girls. I was only interested in computers. They called me a freak, but I didn't care.

I was an only child and a lonely child. But through my computer I met all the friends I wanted. Every night after school I raced through my homework, then sat at my computer screen for four hours or more. A small box at the side of the machine was connected to the phone line and through the phone lines I could exchange messages with friends at the other side of the world.

But Karl was my special computer friend, and now Karl is dead.

I first realized that Karl was local when I switched on my computer one evening in the autumn of 1988 and found an electronic message waiting for me. "Interested in making money from your computer? Contact Karl." And it gave his electronic address. I saw that it was local and I knew I needed money desperately to keep my computer up to date.

I tapped in his address and contacted Karl. At first we exchanged harmless messages and then one evening Karl's message asked, "Why not call round and see me?"

I had contacted hundreds of people over the computer network; I'd never met one face-to-face. Karl's address was just on the other side of Hanover – the side where the wealthy people lived. It was just 20 minutes on a bus. I switched off my computer early that night and left the house.

Karl lived in a flat with security doors at the main entrance. I'd never come across anything like it and pushed nervously at the button marked "Karl Koch".

"Who's there?" asked a tinny voice from the speaker.

"Peter. Peter Ahlen," I said. A buzz sounded from the lock on the door and I pushed it open. I took the lift to the third floor and found him waiting at the door. I guessed he was about 25 years old. He was thin and pale like someone who never saw the sun. He wore round spectacles in wire frames and the eyes behind the glass were never still. We shook hands awkwardly.

"I guess you'll want to see my set-up," he said.

I nodded shyly and he led me through the living-room and into a small room that was lit mainly by the blue-green light from his computer screen. The computer simply amazed me. If I was Aladdin with three wishes I'd have wished for a computer like that. "Show me what you can do," he said.

I hadn't realized I was there for some kind of test, but I sat at the keyboard and found some of my favourite network sites in the USA and Britain. He looked faintly disappointed. "Are you into hacking?"

I took a deep breath. Using the network to steal files from other people's programs is illegal. I knew how to do it – I'd simply never dared. "No," I said, a little ashamed that he'd see me as some sort of wimp.

That night he showed me how to hack – really hack. How to get into secret files by discovering their passwords and reading documents that were a mass of words and figures I didn't understand. It took another three meetings that autumn before I was good enough to do it without his help. In that time we became friends. My first real friend, I guess. And now he's dead.

After a month he gave me his computer. The thought of having that wonderful machine on my own desk took my breath away. "I can't afford it!" I gasped.

"It's a gift," he said. "In future I want you to work from home and do hacking for me. I'm ready to upgrade to a new computer anyway. You may as well have this old one."

"But why? What sort of work?" I asked.

"You've seen the way I hack into company computers?"

"Yes."

"I get information on things like sales figures. If a company does really well then people who have shares in it can make a fortune. The trick is to know a company is doing well *before* the rest of the public know. I simply sell that information to my contacts. It's harmless."

"It's spying. It's illegal," I said.

He looked at me, then his restless eyes flickered away. "It's just a game," he said. "You can make hundreds of Deutschmarks a month."

"Why don't you do it and make the money for yourself?" I asked. "Why give it to me?"

"Because I haven't time for this spying into companies. I

210

have other things to do with my computer time."

"What things?"

He chewed on his lip for a while then said, "Let's see how you get on with this. I'll let you into my little secret another time. OK?"

I shrugged. I was too excited at the idea of making a fortune to think about Karl's schemes. I trusted him. He was my friend, but now he's dead.

My part of the deal worked perfectly. I hacked and stole and sneaked my way into computers around the world to find the information I needed. I loaded it on to floppy disks, passed it to Karl and an envelope stuffed with money arrived within a week. I'd never seen so much money. I didn't dare tell my parents what I was doing and I didn't have anything I wanted to spend the money on. I just pushed it into my dressing-table drawer under my clean socks.

It was like Karl said. A game. Unreal. Until one day I received a message from Karl. "Come and see me. Make sure you're not followed. If anyone is watching my flat then turn around and go home."

We'd been sending messages through the computers for months. It would be strange to see him face to face again.

It was winter now, of course, and snow was drifting down out of a colourless sky as I climbed on the bus. A few people got on the bus at the same stop. More got on and left at various stops along the road. No one got off at the stop nearest Karl's house. Whatever was going on, I was sure I wasn't being followed. A silver Audi car stopped at the end of the road and snapped off its headlights as I stepped off the bus. I guessed they could have followed by car if they had been watching my house.

I stayed at the stop as if I was waiting for another bus to come along. After a few minutes the Audi pulled away and drove past me. I was alone in the street outside Karl's flat. Anyone with any sense was indoors out of the freezing wind. I crossed the road and looked over my shoulder before I pressed the buzzer on the entrance to Karl's block of flats. Anyone could have been watching from any of the darkened windows of the houses opposite. It was a chance I had to take.

The door buzzed and I stepped inside. The warmth of the central heating wrapped itself around me and I took the lift up to the third floor.

Karl was waiting by the door. His face was paler than ever and his expression bleak. Even his restless eyes seemed frozen in some helplessness. "What's wrong?" I asked.

"I've been tricked," he said over his shoulder as he led the way into his computer room. He sat on the swivel chair by the keyboard and rocked slowly backwards and forwards.

"What happened?" I asked.

"I was making a good living from spying on company secrets – the way you are now. But it was too easy," he said and his voice was dull. "I wasn't greedy. I just wanted a challenge. I wanted to hack into the world's greatest secrets just to prove I could do it. Like a mountain climber would want to climb Everest, just to prove themselves."

"What sort of secrets?"

"Military secrets," he said.

And he told me what he'd been doing for the last few months. "I found ways into most of the United States Military research bases. I've hacked into the latest weapon system secrets, into NASA's space programme, into the Central Intelligence Agency's spy network and into the FBI records. There is hardly a secret in the USA that I couldn't get at sooner or later."

"And Russia and China?" I asked.

He turned away from me. "No, not them."

Suddenly I understood. "You've been spying *for* the Russians? Passing your data to their spies?"

"The KGB," he nodded.

"And now you've been found out?"

"I … I think so. I never stayed connected to a secret file too long. I didn't want the Americans to be able to trace me. Then I came across a new, huge batch of secrets in a file called SDINET. It would take me a long time to load that file on to my computer, but the KGB ordered me to do it."

"Even if it meant you getting caught?"

"They said they'd protect me."

"You think the Americans are on to you now? Then ask the KGB to help," I said. I couldn't see the problem.

"It seems this SDINET information was rubbish. It was just

a collection of old, useless material. It was just cheese in a trap and I was the mouse. The KGB are furious – the CIA are on their way to get me, they reckon, and Russia doesn't want to get the blame. I'm on my own."

"That's awful!" I cried.

"I was well paid – while it lasted," he sighed. "Now I have to take my punishment. Quite a few years in jail. But that's not why I asked you to come around."

In the next hour he showed me how to destroy all the memory on the computer I had back at home. "The CIA will want to know my contacts. I've wiped out every trace of you on this computer. You need to do the same at your end. Understand?"

"Yes, Karl. Thanks."

He gave a weak smile. "There's no point in us both being dragged down. Now go, destroy that information, but make sure no one is following you."

I rose to leave. "Is there no way to save yourself?" I asked.

"I'm a computer spy – an armchair agent. I'm not one of the spies you read about in books – on the run with a poison capsule under my tongue and a gun in my pocket. I wouldn't know where to start. No, Peter. If you can save yourself I'll be happy. Good luck."

We shook hands one last time and I let myself out into the winter night.

For the next month my parents were amazed to find me leaving my computer every night to watch the television news. It was January before a serious newsreader announced, "German police have uncovered a computer spy ring in Hanover that is alleged to have stolen thousands of secret documents electronically and passed them on to KGB Agents in Berlin..."

The police were taking the credit but everyone knew the American Secret Service were behind the arrests. I followed the case in the newspapers and was relieved to see they released Karl at Easter before he came to trial in May. If he was free to return home they can't have thought he was such a dangerous criminal after all.

It all seemed so hopeful. My spirits raised and I even tried a little computer hacking, just for fun.

When the news came through that he had failed to report to the police, I cheered. He had made a run for it at last – his KGB friends must have finally helped him out, I decided.

Then, a week later, he was found. What was left of him. The reporter said police were treating it as suicide. His car was found abandoned in a lonely wood. Near by they saw Karl's charred body. It had been soaked in petrol and set on fire.

There were murmurs about this being a strange form of suicide. Who would want to die horribly like that? But no one mentioned the word "murder".

I read every newspaper report, word for word, and even used my computer to sift through the details. Look at them for yourself. He died with no shoes on and no shoes in the car – who would drive 20 miles without shoes?

There were scorch marks round the body but nowhere else – had he lain perfectly still while he burned?

His contacts in the computer spy ring had given all they knew to the police and knew that in return they would go free – so why on earth would Karl want to kill himself?

I've thought about it and worried about it for ten years now. I know that he was murdered. Spying is a dangerous business and failures often die. I know my friend was murdered. There's just one thing I don't know: which side killed him? The Americans or the Russians?

Somewhere, hidden deep in a computer file in Moscow or in Washington, there is the answer. The only way I'll ever find out is if I get into that file and read it. I'm as good at hacking now as Karl ever was. I'm ready to start searching for the truth from the comfort of my armchair in front of this keyboard. I'm ready to become a hacker and a spy. Karl would like that.

If I disappear, then end up a blackened corpse, you'll know I've failed. But I have to try.

After all, Karl was my friend, and now he's dead.

Spying today is not what it was when agents were dropped by parachutes into enemy territory or lived in enemy camps and slipped coded messages out. Today spies need different skills…

1. Computer hacking. If enemies can connect their computers to your computer then they can read all the secrets you've stored. In 1975, the US Navy was worried about enemy agents "hacking" into its computer, so it decided to spy on itself! "Tiger" teams were set up, who had to try and hack into the navy's most secret files. The tiger teams broke into, and took over, every single computer system they tried to enter.

2. Computer viruses. If you can't read an enemy's secret files then the next best thing you can do is destroy them so he can't read them either. Some computer programs can be fed into an enemy computer to wipe out the records or change them so the computer gives out false commands that confuse the enemy.

3. Computer bugs. America's Federal Bureau of Investigation (FBI) used a bug to find a traitor in their country's Central Intelligence Agency. From 1985 the man, Aldrich Ames, had been giving the Russians the names of American spies and at least ten of them died as a result.

FACT FILE

TOP SECRET

The FBI won't say how they uncovered his treachery, but it is believed the keyboard of his computer was fitted with a special bug. Every key he tapped sent a signal to an FBI computer so they got instant copies of all his letters as soon as he wrote them. In 1994 he was arrested and went to prison for life.

4. Spy satellites. Spies no longer need to cross borders to get the pictures they need. In 1959 the USA began using cameras in satellites to take pictures over enemy territory. They were simple things at first – the camera took a roll of film, the film was ejected, parachuted down to the Pacific Ocean and snatched in mid-air by a US aeroplane. (It couldn't be reloaded but 1,000 metres of film showed 1.6 million square miles of Soviet territory!) Now cameras beam pictures directly back to earth and can spot items as small as one metre across; heat image cameras can also see objects five metres *below* the sands of the Sahara Desert.

5. Satellite bugs. There is no need for a spy to break into an enemy's office and plant a bug. Spy satellites can now fly high over the target and pick up radio and telephone messages on the ground below.

Is this the end of the spy? Will he or she just become some computer expert sitting behind a desk and learning everything they need to know from spy machines?

Look at what happened in the Gulf War in 1991. Iraq, led by Saddam Hussein, invaded the country next door – Kuwait.

Britain and America went to the aid of Kuwait and drove the invaders back. They used all the spy equipment available to help their armies, navies and air forces drive the Iraqis back. Spy satellites told the British and US armies exactly where Iraqi troops were moving and guided missiles and bombs on to targets.

But remember, the spy satellites didn't warn the US and British that the Iraqis were planning an invasion. It would have needed a man or woman close to Saddam Hussein's headquarters to warn of that. It would have needed a human spy. Their days are not over yet.

EPILOGUE

Spying isn't what it used to be. Spies aren't what they used to be.

In the past no one except the spies' masters knew who they were or where they worked. You couldn't just walk up to spy headquarters and apply for a job. You would not expect to see an advert in a newspaper saying, "Spies wanted."

But now you *can*!

In May 1997 the British Military Intelligence Agency put an advert in national newspapers and it invited people to apply for a job with them. Spies have been caught and suffered horrible deaths – tortured, shot, hanged and poisoned. Who on earth would want a job like that? Well, in the first week after the advert appeared more than 20,000 people applied.

If the 20,000 who applied think they are going to end up like James Bond, then they will be disappointed. The "super-powers" of the United States and Russia are at peace. In the 1960s they raced to be the first nation to have rockets in space. Now the American astronauts and Russian cosmonauts share a space station and work side by side. No more space-race secrets and no need for spies to steal those secrets.

America is also very open about its spy operations these days. Central Intelligence Agency files are open to anyone in the world on the Internet. Every week 120,000 people connect to the CIA site on:

http://www.odci.gov/cia/index.html

and more connect to the FBI on HYPERLINK:

http://www.fbi.gov

Of course the CIA has its own "Internet" for the *really* secret material that the public can't read.

But there *are* still enemies at work and there *are* still secrets that need to be protected or uncovered. There are terrorists who want to assassinate leaders and destroy cities. There are drug dealers who want to smuggle dangerous substances and destroy lives. There are international criminals who smuggle everything from money and jewels to computer software and people. The police work hard to stop them, but it is so much easier if they know what these enemies of the state are planning next. We still need spies.

And spying is still terribly dangerous. Suppose a spy pretends to be a terrorist and finds out where they are hiding weapons – he or she will somehow have to pass on that information to the law officers. If he or she is caught passing on that information then the terrorists are not likely to be merciful.

Some things never change. As long as there are evil people planning harm to us then we need spies to help us stop them. Spies have always been seen as ruthless people who can't be trusted. But the truth is, spies can be the best friends we could ever wish for.